START
AGAIN

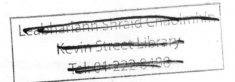

ALSO BY PHILIP COLLINS

When They Go Low, We Go High

Philip Collins

START
AGAIN

How We Can Fix
Our Broken Politics

4th ESTATE • *London*

4th Estate
An imprint of HarperCollins*Publishers*
1 London Bridge Street
London SE1 9GF

www.4thEstate.co.uk

First published in Great Britain in 2018 by 4th Estate

1

Copyright © Philip Collins, 2018

Philip Collins asserts the moral right to be identified
as the author of this work in accordance with the
Copyright, Designs and Patents Act 1988

A catalogue record for this book is
available from the British Library

ISBN 978-0-00-831264-0

Printed and bound in Great Britain by
CPI Group (UK) Ltd, Croydon

MIX
Paper from
responsible sources
FSC® C007454

This book is produced from independently certified FSC paper
to ensure responsible forest management.

For more information visit: www.harpercollins.co.uk/green

To Geeta, with love and thanks

CONTENTS

PROLOGUE

THE POLITICAL
VIRTUES

A Political Home

Sir Robert Peel died a fêted man. On 10 July 1850, eight days after he fell from his horse to a sudden death, a public meeting in the court house at Bury Town Hall resolved to erect a monument as a memorial to 'our eminent townsman'. A Testimonial Committee was appointed and £2,700 was crowd-funded, from 2,000 contributors. An exhibition was staged in February 1851 for the public to inspect the mooted statuettes, busts and architectural designs. Though the venue forbade entry to 'Persons in Clogs', the working people of Bury ran up the steps in their stockinged-feet, close to 15,000 of them, to see the designs. Much the same number attended the inauguration of Edward Hodges Baily's finished statue on 8 September 1852, in the company of Sir Robert's son, Frederick Peel, MP for Bury.

Robert Peel was held in such esteem because he was thought to have spoken plainly in the hope of improving the condition of the people. Can anybody imagine today the stockinged-footed legions rushing to the municipal hall to approve plans to commemorate a politician? Right now, nobody is putting politicians on a pedestal.

The greatest political son of my home town has stood in bronze since 1852, surveying the public space outside the Parish Church of St Mary the Virgin. The statue of Peel depicts the Bury Prime Minister clad in contemporary dress, speaking to the House of Commons about the high price of bread that made life such a misery for the urban poor. On the statue's granite pedestal, a circular bronze panel contains lines from the speech in which Peel announced his resignation as Prime Minister on 29 June 1846. 'It may be, I shall leave a name', the inscription reads, 'sometimes remembered with expressions of goodwill in the abode of those whose lot it is to labour, and to earn their daily bread by the sweat of their brow – when they shall recruit their exhausted strength with abundant and untaxed food the sweeter because it is no longer leavened by a sense of injustice'.

These are words that speak both to and about the people. Peel was talking about the twin virtues of British democratic politics at its best; it grants power to the people and it provides them, fairly, with benefits. Peel knew that his action would be likely to split the Conservative party but he proceeded all the same. His memorial in Bury is a reminder that good politics can redeem its promise. It is far from doing so now.

Today in Britain there is a legion of people without a political home. I am one of them. I grew up in a staunchly Conservative family in Robert Peel's town of Bury. But rebellious like Peel himself, I split from the family allegiance because the Social Democratic Party (SDP) seemed like a novel answer to Britain's mood of decline. Even at a young age the discipline of the Tories wedded to the romance of Labour seemed to me like the perfect compound rather than the terms of the fight. When the SDP collapsed in 1988, I joined the Labour party. I did so for the same reason that most people do. I wanted to make the world better. If that sounds naive then it is deliberately so. I believed at the time, and I believe now, that good politics can be the agent of the good society and, unlike my grandfather, who always saw the Conservative party as the vehicle of progress, I found that energy in the Labour party. I soon learnt that too much of that energy was poorly directed. This was a time, the mid-1980s, when the far left had taken control of the party. My first job in politics was for Frank Field who had been deselected as MP for Birkenhead by the entryist group Socialist Organiser. The antics of the far left taught me an unforgettable political lesson. When people become convinced of their own righteousness the last thing they are capable of being is righteous. The politics were masculine and vicious. Claiming to act in the name of working people, the left achieved nothing beyond confirming its own purity. Today the same people are back. The Labour party has fallen victim to a juvenile anti-capitalism and loathing of America. A party too hospitable to conspiracy theories, chief among them anti-Semitism, is, sadly, no longer a noble institution.

The Conservative party, meanwhile, has dragged the nation into its own private feud. Fired by too pure an account of sovereignty, the party is in the process, whimsically and chaotically, of taking Britain out of the EU for reasons it can barely remember let alone define. The split instigated by Peel over the Corn Laws opened a fault line in Conservative thought between trade and protectionism, between being open to the world and being closed off. That fault line has run through all of the party's travails over Europe and, at last, it is yielding to the temptation to raise the drawbridge. It is a deeply inadequate response to a world in which connections are more extensive and more important than ever before.

The two main parties have retreated inwards and the brand of the Liberal Democrats is fatally tarnished. They are both indulging themselves in what they really think, unconcerned that what they really think is not what the nation really needs. When neither party can honour the two virtues of British politics, the country needs new leadership and new ideas. The bronze memorial to Sir Robert Peel in Bury stands today as a reproach to a political class with nothing important to say. There is no sense of popular power and the results, measured in material progress, have ceased to flow. It is time to start again.

Three Life Stories

But in order to start again we need to understand what we have lost. To understand *that* we need to know how we gained it in the first place. The story of the promise of politics can be told through three family tales which start and end where Peel stands, in Bury.

In 1788, in Chamber Hall in Bury, a boy was born into the calico-printing fortune of the local mill-owner. Throughout the odyssey of this young man's life, via Bury Grammar School, Harrow, Oxford University, the House of Commons and 10 Downing Street, he retained a distinct regional accent and was regularly disparaged for cutting his jelly with a knife. He will forever be known, and to my mind admired, for breaking the mould of British politics. Today, as well as standing guard in bronze over his home town, Sir Robert Peel lends his name to the by-pass, the health centre, a public house and the 128-foot tower which was inaugurated the day after Peel's statue and which overlooks the town from Holcombe Hill.

Peel had great intellectual gifts and an ardent work ethic but he was lucky enough to be born into a fortune. In time, life chances became more meritocratic. By no means fully and by no means everywhere, but often enough for it to seem that effort plus ability, the meritocratic formula, could secure the good life. The second Bury story begins on the threshold of one world war and spans another. This is the tale of a man born in 1910, within sight of Walshaw Hall, the seat of the weaving entrepreneur James Kenyon, Conservative MP for Bury. This child stayed in his town through school, work and retirement. Though evidently bright enough for higher education, he left school at fifteen, to work in the textile industry whose presence in the town owed so much to Robert Peel's father. This man worked fifty years for James Kenyon, rising from office boy to foreman. On the day he retired he had his picture in the *Bury Times* clutching a gold clock and shaking hands with the boss.

The name of this man was Thomas Taylor and he was my grandfather. Adamantine, conservative and thirsty for the knowledge he memorised from the encyclopaedia, he became a church warden and a school governor. Tom Taylor was a man of granite decency and he was a meritocrat. He worked inordinately hard, entering every penny he earned and spent in double ledgers in his book of accounts. My grandfather took great pride in the work that was his source of welfare, both material and spiritual. I have, fading on my desk before me as I write these words, a photograph, of me as a boy with the man who launched my family's journey towards the place from which I am now writing these reflections.

My grandfather's story is the platform on which the protagonist of the third tale stands. It is the beginning of my story. The security my grandfather built, in the last era in which manufacturing industry was a sure road to prosperity, he passed on to his daughter. The legacy included a devotion to the Church of England, a respect for education and a moral code for life. It also included a life-long and ardent allegiance to the Conservative party, membership of which my grandfather saw as both a signal that he had ascended the social scale and a guarantee that greater progress was possible. He regarded the Labour party's stress on equality as proclaiming its intention to hold him back.

The year after I was born, James Kenyon & Son was taken over by the Albany Felt Company of Albany, New York. It was a sign that power had passed from our town. As a boy I played in the derelict, dangerous Peel Mill, searching for the resident tramp of our fevered imaginations. It was a palatial structure that retained its grandeur even though the clatter of looms had long gone. There is nothing there now. The dog-walkers and runners on the banks of the River Irwell would never guess, if they did not know, that a castle of the first Industrial Revolution once stood here.

My mother was never destined for Peel Mill. She spent her working life fulfilling the only ambition she ever had which was to be a primary school teacher. She taught me too and that was the start of the journey through the town's grammar school and on to higher education that made it possible for me to leave Bury for the rest of the world. I grew up in a household that had its dinner at what I would now call lunchtime and in which tea was a meal as well as a drink. Nobody went out for dinner and, if they had, it would have happened in the middle of the day. In the vanishingly unlikely event that we had been invited out for supper, my parents would have expected a cup of cocoa and a biscuit. From there I went on a journey through the English class system, through the doors of the great British institutions, always nervous but never less than excited: Cambridge University, the House of Commons, the BBC, the City of London, 10 Downing Street, *The Times*.

Next to the picture of my grandfather I have on my desk a photograph of my mother, with my two boys, aged four and two at the time, in the Downing Street rose garden in 2006. My mother liked to embarrass me with the story that, the night before I was born, she dreamt of Harold Wilson, whom she could not abide. It was my fitting revenge that the daughter of Thomas Taylor, herself a life-long Conservative, should find herself at the summer party thrown by Tony Blair, a Labour Prime Minister. Mr Blair always asked what my mum thought of policies. That was because she was from Bury, a town that always picked the winner in a general election. It was a moment of great pride, even if she did regard my unaccountable decision to swap sides as enough to make Peel step down from his pedestal. There was never a day, when I knocked on the famous black door to enter Downing Street, that I did not reflect on the privilege. I feel the same when I open a copy of *The Times* and find my script offered to the nation under a flattering picture taken some time ago. I like to think my grandfather might have been proud of that, even if he would have been dubious about my political affiliation.

This is my story and many others could once tell a similar story of their own. It is, though, today a rarer story than it was, and that is evidence of the broken promise of British politics. It was once assumed that every succeeding generation would do materially better than the one that went before. Parents would hand on to children a world enhanced and improved. Sir Robert Peel's two political virtues offered power and progress to the people. My grandfather found secure employment in manufacturing which, through dedicated husbandry, he turned into opportunities that my mother took and passed on to me. This was, though the connection was never conscious, the contract between the political class and the electorate it served.

The Story of Modernisation

This book tells how that contract can be reinstated. The story of politics is the story of constant modernisation. A political movement courts success only when it looks like the future arriving. Clement Attlee promised that the sacrifice of war would be repaid by the benefits of welfare. Harold Wilson pledged to make Britain comfortable in the white heat of the technological revolution. Tony Blair spoke the language of globalisation and the coming information age. All three, in their own ways, said that their politics would shape and domesticate the future. Today, in an economy in which too many people miss out, in which unmerited rewards flow freely and in which work seems to be threatened by the next wave of industrial revolution there is an urgent need for a political movement that sounds like the cavalry of the future taking the field.

I begin with a definition of what has gone awry but the main focus of the book has to be time future rather than time past. No new dispensation is possible, however, without a clear understanding of time present and, in 'The Broken Promise', the first chapter, I chart the terrain. Politics over the last decade has been operating under new terms and conditions. When the next generation cannot reasonably expect any improvement on the living standards of their parents, then the implicit political bargain has broken down. This is the troubling context in which Britain faces, I go on to suggest, ten pressing questions to which the current set of politicians has no answers. First, there are the economic questions of how Britain makes a living in the world, how we tackle inequalities of income and wealth, the most conspicuous of which has become the allocation of housing, and how we reassure the workforce that technology is not a mortal threat. Then there are the political questions of how we restore faith in public deliberation, the location of power and how we improve life chances by devising public services that both enhance the citizen body and respect justice between the generations. Last come the vital cultural questions of providing a home for all, ensuring that Britain remains a tolerant and open society and defining Britain's place in the world.

The rest of the book seeks to answer those questions. It will set out the principles and the policies to design what I shall call the new common wealth of Great Britain. This is an idea with a deep heritage in the best of the various traditions of British political thought but it melds them to form something new. The common wealth will put an enterprising economy at the service of an open society to create a liberal democracy of which we can be proud.

The fundamental fact of recent British politics is that the average British worker has not had a pay rise for a decade. This has bled into a more general critique of modern capitalism and its unfair and unequal distribution of rewards. In chapter 2, 'The Common Wealth', I return to the origins of modern capitalism in the public obligation of the corporate enterprise. An economy in which the fruits are more evenly spread is, I argue, not only a present-day necessity, it is also a way of honouring the history of capitalism and therefore of protecting an open economy against its enemies. This will require a system of taxation which is based on principles of desert and earned income.

The next task is to manage the same recuperation for the reputation of politics. The advertised and formidable benefits of democracy are that people are granted sovereign power and that their world gets better. The two virtues are linked at the deepest level. The world improves, in part, because people feel a sense of agency. However, British politics has fallen into a rut in which neither of these two benefits are accruing. The purpose of chapter 3, 'The Liberal Democracy', is therefore to describe a state apparatus that can both command widespread popular assent and start, once again, to work efficiently on behalf of the citizen body. This will mean, in one of the most centralised states in the democratic world, that power will need to be deployed at a far lower level. It is often noted that the people no longer have much trust in politicians. This is true, but not as telling as it sounds. The far greater problem is that politicians have not trusted the people.

The relationship between the citizen and the state is enacted in the public services. The ways we educate our children, treat our sick or care for our needy are not just important transactions in which we exchange vital goods. The organisational choices and spending priorities that we make are ways to embody an idea of who we are. The ethos of public service which informs our public relationships with one another defines a public realm. In chapter 4, 'Power Failure', I set out the principles of control, capability, prevention and contribution that should govern the way we provide vital services.

We live a life in common with others when we meet in public places but to live in common with other people is also an act of imagination. When there is an identity between the country we hold in our minds and the country we hold in prospect, then that nation is likely to be content. Division is inevitable in the sense that a democracy will always be home to plural views. These views have to be settled, though, in a civil way, and that entails agreement on certain basic rules and structures. When the claims of particular identities are too strong, common life gets pulled apart. In chapter 5, 'The Open Society', I will describe the nation that we should want Britain to be, a conception of a country that asks neither too much nor too little of any of its citizens of many faiths and many cultures.

These five chapters seek to define and then answer the questions that will determine the next phase of Britain's course as a nation. It sketches a new common wealth for Britain. Throughout the book there runs an assumption that the nation needs a jolt, an electric surge to galvanise its politics. It is drifting into a position that shuts it away from the world. Unsure of its place and its status, an old country is in danger of fading from view. Neither of the two main political parties has any inkling of how to stop this slow dissolve. The Conservative party has fallen into Peel's chasm between open trade and a closed nation. The Labour party has retreated into its nostrum that all the deficiencies of public services can be met by spending the money it has no idea how it can raise.

Above and beyond the two dominant parties, a large tract of political ground lies unoccupied. A band of political orphans has been created. These are the people to whom and for whom this book purports to speak. Half the electorate say that no party speaks for them and that they would consider switching their vote if there were a credible third option available. More than that say no party speaks for them. These political orphans come from all strata of society and all age groups. They lean both to the right and to the left, though none too far. Their sense of lacking a home is itself an indictment of the recent conduct of British politics. The archaic and undignified British constitution is cracking. Power is hoarded by a distant and unresponsive centre and local outposts, despite the few recent innovations of mayoralties, remain vestigial and weak. This is a political dispensation in which neither of the two advertised virtues arrives as stated. Neither agency nor benefits are in evidence. It is surely time for us to start again.

1

THE BROKEN
PROMISE

The Fall of the Meritocracy

Eight miles from where Peel stands outside Bury Parish Church is one of Britain's most important democratic sites. St Peter's Field is the location of the Peterloo massacre of 1819, the occasion when the authorities reacted to the popular demand for parliamentary representation and better living standards by sending in the militia. It then became the place where Richard Cobden built the Free Trade Hall to commemorate the radical liberal victory over the Corn Laws that caused Peel to fracture the Conservative party.

This was where Michael Young, the chief author of the 1945 Labour party manifesto, chose to set his fictional dystopia *The Rise of the Meritocracy*. Young does not coin the term *meritocracy* as a compliment. His book is a warning about what can happen when a smug elite starts to believe that its good fortune is merited. The story ends, in the far distant year of 2033, with the death of the narrator at the hands of the revolting plebeians. The historical journey of St Peter's Field begins with a protest to demand popular sovereignty and cheaper bread and ends in a civil war of the people against the elite.

Britain is today divided old against young, class against class, region against region, nativist against cosmopolitan, rich against poor, and London against the rest. It is a country divided by generation, by level of education, by place and by attitude. The referendum on British membership of the EU in June 2016 exposed, though it did not create, these rifts in British life. Seventy-one per cent of voters under the age of twenty-four wanted to stay in. Sixty-four per cent of voters over the age of sixty-five wanted to leave. People in the professions voted to stay; unskilled workers voted to leave. People who cite inequality as a major preoccupation were for in; those who said immigration counted most were for out. London, Manchester and Liverpool voted to stay and so did most of Scotland. Every other region, the towns and villages of England, fell the other way.

In *The Condition of the Working Class in England*, launched into the tempest of the Corn Law dispute in 1845, the Manchester mill-owner Friedrich Engels argued that the Industrial Revolution, which had enriched the owners of capital, had done nothing for the people who lived and worked in the industrial cities. In *Sybil*, the novel he wrote in response to Engels, Disraeli coined the phrase 'two nations' to describe the division between the rich and the poor. The very message that

Engels telegraphed first time around is now coming back again from the post-industrial revolution. It is a big question: the condition of England question or, rather, the condition of Britain question, and today there is not just one of them but ten.

We will come, in the chapters that follow, to the principles, methods and policies that could start to furnish answers but we need, before that, to state the problems baldly. These are the problems that every political party will face whether it has answers or not. The price of having nothing to say is that the country carries on drifting, with no direction, endlessly, to nowhere in particular.

Ten Condition of Britain Questions

The ten condition of Britain questions fall into three categories, the first of which is the income and wealth of the nation. The distribution of wealth becomes less fair with every passing year and earnings growth has disappeared. This has broken the covenant of British housing and shut out a generation of prospective buyers. Then there is the chronic threat that automation is said to pose to the structure of developed economies. All these anxieties together conjure a fear about how Britain will earn its living. The second set of questions are political. British institutions are not working well. They do not grant the citizens a sense of agency and they are not providing services either fairly or of adequate quality. The third and final body of questions are cultural. With Britain on the cusp of breaking its relationship with the EU it will need to find a new sense of ease and a new place in the world.

Taken together, these are the fundamental facts of contemporary British politics. They help to explain Britain's European decision, the strangely volatile aberration of the general election of 2017 and the appeal of the populism of Jeremy Corbyn. Leaving the EU in turn intensifies the problem. There is no assessment of the medium-term economic outlook that does not describe leaving as an economic loss. This simply redoubles the importance of the first pressing condition of Britain question, which is how Britain makes its way in the world.

1 How Does Britain Make a Living?

The first industrial nation has slowly transformed itself into a viable service economy. It does, however, lack many sectors of world-class calibre. One industry in which Britain competes at world class causes as many problems as it provides solutions. The banking crisis of 2008 showed the fragility of an economy which is too heavily reliant on financial services. A vast tranche of public money was, rightly, committed to rescuing the banking system. Had the bail-out not been forthcoming the consequences would have been even worse than they were. As it was, they were merely dreadful. The deficit in the public finances rose, at its height, to £103 billion, which is 6.9 per cent of GDP, the highest since the Second World War.

Tax revenue was revealed to be too concentrated in the City of London. Financial services accounted for 14 per cent of all tax collected in 2007 and today they still account for 11 per cent. The excessive reliance on financial services is also a way of describing an economy that is geographically unbalanced. The towns and cities of Britain outside London rose out of the ashes of manufacturing during the 1980s, but the recovery was deceptive. It was based too heavily on public spending and a reinvigorated public sector. A third of the jobs in Newcastle in 2017 were in the public sector. When the banks crashed they spread chaos into the system and the nasty medicine of austerity made the condition worse. The private sector in London and the public sector in Newcastle were shown to be umbilically linked.

Yet it would be self-harming to denigrate the financial services industry to the point that it flees. Britain is already taking that risk by leaving the EU and further hostility would be foolish. The rules of the British economy require a great deal of change, on which more anon, but the nation can only grow, can only answer all the questions that follow, if its economy is productive. To begin that process by dismantling a globally competitive industry would be an eccentric move. The tough question though remains: if Britain is not to be over-reliant on finance and if it is not going to use public spending as its method of economic recovery, where is the enterprise and what will the people of Britain do and make? Unless there is a clear route to prosperity the question of the distribution of wealth becomes redundant. But as long as there is no such route, then that is the second pressing economic question we face.

2 How Do We Reduce Inequalities of Income and Wealth?

Each generation born after 1955 has accumulated less than the one that went before. The ownership of property has also declined with every succeeding generation since the 1950s, and so has net financial wealth in the form of current and savings accounts, equities and gilts. The richest 10 per cent of people in Britain now own 66 per cent of the nation's wealth. Glacially but surely, the pattern of reward in capitalism has shifted towards the mill-owner and away from the foreman, let alone the worker on the shop floor. Over the last four decades the share of national value which has gone into the pay packet has fallen from 59 per cent to 54 per cent. The suppliers of capital have seen their share rise from 22 per cent to 27 per cent.

This would matter less if everyone was being paid more, but alas they are not. The promissory note of British politics was that higher labour productivity would be rewarded with higher pay. All over the developed world that link has broken. It broke abruptly in the United States in 1970. Median earnings in Canada have been flat for thirty years, even though productivity has grown by

37 per cent. Real monthly income fell over the past decade in Germany. Mechanisation and the premium paid for skilled over unskilled work has now broken the link in Britain. Wage growth has been lagging productivity improvements for two decades. In the five years before the recession of 2008 the economy grew more than 2 per cent each year and productivity by 1.6 per cent each year. But the workers did not get paid for their smarter work. Median incomes were flat apart from at the top, where they kept rising. Until 2002, average wages grew in tandem with GDP. Not now: average wages stopped growing in 2003 and are not expected to pick up before 2020.

Deprived of pay progression, most people now earn what they might have expected to earn ten years ago. A decade has been spirited away. The young have had it even worse; for people in their mid-twenties, fifteen years of pay growth have disappeared. Nearly half of the people affected have no qualifications beyond GCSEs. They spend a lot of their disposable income on food and petrol and two-thirds of them are not saving a penny for their pension. It is quite possible that the fortunes of those who start work in a time of stagnant pay growth will never fully recover. These are the people for whom housing takes up too much of their income and whose hopes of ever becoming home-owners are receding. Housing is the third urgent question.

3 How Do We Provide a Home for All?

Housing has often been the point at which public policy and the political promise meet. After the Great War, David Lloyd George pledged to redeem the sacrifice of the conflict with homes fit for the returning heroes. Neville Chamberlain summarised the Conservative promise to the nation as the creation of a 'property-owning democracy'. After the Second World War, Aneurin Bevan's reputation came at least as much from the housing stock that was built as it did from the formation of the NHS. Margaret Thatcher's popularity with the urban working class came in large part because she adopted a policy that Frank Field had proposed but the Labour party had rejected — the sale of council houses to their tenants.

Housing is once again a pivotal question in British politics because a generation is being locked out. At the start of the last century only 10 per cent of the nation owned their own home. By the end of the century home ownership had risen to 70 per cent. George Orwell was one of the first writers to comment on the way the Englishman made a castle of his home. The British cultivated a peculiar relationship with the residential home, which they have treated as both somewhere to live and a principal investment at the same time — a decision encouraged by advantageous taxation. This was the process by which a generation of people bought their own homes and, understandably, passed them down the family line. At the same time, the number of households increased as the population grew, people married later, divorced more often and lived longer. Land was too tightly controlled, which meant that house builders hung on to it because it kept growing in value. When the supply of new houses failed to keep pace with demand, the obvious consequence was a boost in the price of property. Those already in the market have prospered but those who have yet to gain entry may now never do so. Britain faces the genuine likelihood, for the first time in its modern history, that people who are thirty years of age may never own their own home, even though they are in stable and relatively well-paid work. Someone who is thirty years of age today, who saves 5 per cent of his disposable income every year, will put down a deposit on a house of average price in the year he turns seventy-five. House prices have doubled relative to income over his lifetime.

This is a generational shift of a fundamental kind because no part of the British political promise has been more important, or more constantly repeated, than the pledge of a home. As a result, the private rental sector is fragmented and of disreputable quality. Housing has now become a crisis of the first order, every bit as important as it was after either of the two world wars. When the people feel they are not getting a fair deal from policy – which on housing they are not – we ought not to be surprised when resentment turns into hostility. It could yet get worse for this group of people because those who have suffered pay stagnation, and who are struggling to pay for housing, work in food services, retail, construction, information technology and manufacturing, exactly the sorts of trades most at risk from the threat of automation. This brings us to the fourth condition of Britain question.

4 How Do We Make Technology Work for Us?

The dystopian vision of work in the future is prosperity without people. The trends that have generated income and wealth inequality will be accelerated. Automation threatens to funnel rewards to the owners of capital as human labour is replaced by technology. Every previous revolution in technology has increased productivity and therefore prosperity while, at the same time, creating a new set of opportunities for work. The fear is that the rule of the robots will be different. A cloud hangs over the future of work; a cloud in cyber-space, annexing all of the routine functions on which an economy depends.

There are plenty of studies like the latest one from the Organisation for Economic Co-operation and Development (OECD), in which it is estimated that half of all jobs, across thirty-two countries, stand at some degree of risk from automation. The Bank of England has calculated that a third of all jobs in Britain face a high risk and a further third face a moderate risk. This accounts for 15 million jobs in total, an apocalyptic forecast with no precedent. Of course, fears about the damage that technology will do to employment go back as far as the wheel. The Industrial Revolution, which brought prosperity to Bury, prompted anxiety, which was in the event unfounded, that human labour would be systematically displaced by machines. We have always adapted before, but perhaps the age of automation will be different. Progress in computing capacity has been truly astonishing. Genius machines can do complex mathematics, medical diagnosis, select stocks for a mutual fund portfolio and beat Garry Kasparov at chess. It may be that the combination of immense labour power in robots that never tire and the artificial brain capacity they now purvey will change all the economic rules.

In previous industrial revolutions the threat was confined to work done by hand. The threat of the revolution to come is that work done by brain is also colonised. The immediate threat, though, is to administrative, clerical and production tasks, precisely those that tend to command the lowest wages. This raises, in turn, the fear that automation intensifies material inequality. The more that an industry is mechanised the more its rewards accrue to the owners of capital and the less to the bearers of labour. This would be disastrous in the pursuit of equal life chances for all. This is the fifth condition of Britain question.

5 How Can We Improve Life Chances?

My grandfather was born in 1910 and died in 1994. During his lifetime, Britain changed from manufacturing to service, from blue-collar to white. When he was born, fewer than a fifth of all jobs were classified in the top two social tiers. By the time he died, two-fifths were. This is the story of John Braine's 1957 novel *Room at the Top*, in which we follow Joe Lampton through the tiered class system. Like Fielding's *Tom Jones*, Joe Lampton is an orphan but, unlike Tom Jones, Joe does not turn out to have been of noble birth all along. He gets there by his own effort and his own talent. For a generation, the Joe Lamptons kept on coming.

But then, not long after my grandfather retired, a disaster hit our town as it did so many others of its type. The textile mills closed and too many of the fathers of my generation were signed off on the sick. Unemployment is a contagion; half the children in Britain with unemployed fathers are unemployed adults themselves now. In Bury, manufacturing declined rapidly. There are wards in the town, among the 10 per cent most deprived in the country, in which a fifth of the people are out of work.

I am fortunate that mine is a story of social mobility. Having joined the bourgeoisie through education, I confirmed my place through marriage. As a child I don't recall ever meeting a doctor unless I was ill. My wife comes from a family that barely knew anyone who wasn't a doctor. From a desirable London postcode close to Milbourne House, where Fielding wrote *Tom Jones*, we now do our best to ensure that our own children have a head start in the race of life. In 1693 John Locke wrote a parenting guide called *Some Thoughts Concerning Education*, in which he recommended that children need eat no vegetables but should take care to be born to the right parents. Locke was a better developmental psychologist than he was a dietician. The children of a pair of professionals will, by the age of three, have heard a million more words than the offspring of less articulate parents. On their first day at school, children from poorer homes turn up less literate, numerate and articulate than their richer peers.

During the era in which the growth of professions such as law and accountancy was creating more room at the top, it was possible for British politics to offer a welcome social mobility in which some went up but nobody fell down. We need to remember that it was never really social engineering that did the work of mobility in Britain. It was civil engineering. Unless our time witnesses a rapid expansion in the fields of biotechnology, nano-technology and artificial intelligence, then the rise of one daughter of the working class is going to require the fall of a son of the bourgeoisie. What Gore Vidal said of friendship is now true of life chances in Britain: 'it is not enough that you should succeed. Others must fail.'

The most vivid image of British society during the twentieth century is to imagine a race run twice, once in 1900 and then again in 2000. All the participants run faster than they did a century ago. The winners and losers, though, are essentially the same. A child born middle-class today is fifteen times more likely to have remained a middle-class adult than a child born work-ing-class. A man who is forty today is more likely to stay in his father's social class than his equivalent born a generation before. He is also, for a series of complex reasons, likely to enjoy a less prosperous life than his father did. Justice between the generations is the next question the country faces.

6 How Do We Ensure Justice between the Generations?

Walshaw Hall, once the grand pile of James Kenyon, is now a residential care home. Britain is growing older and a society so elderly presents political problems of a sort no nation has ever before encountered. A new line is being drawn: old against young. It is not true, as it is sometimes alleged, that my mother's generation, born just before, during and after the Second World War, have purloined the assets or stolen the future. Cohorts do not act consciously as a single cunning alliance and, besides, ensuring dignity in old age is one of Britain's biggest concerns. The provision of social care, for example, does not currently respect this principle.

The flow of assets towards my mother's generation has largely been an effect of size. The doubling in education spending between 1953 and 1973 occurred because of the boom in babies that needed schooling. Those babies have now grown up and, in the strange way that the end of life mimics the start, need looking after again. The growth in life expectancy, from fifty-one for men and fifty-five for women born in 1910 to seventy-nine for men and eighty-three for women today, means that more of the large generation have survived into old age and expensive infirmity. This is why NHS spending keeps increasing. This is why pensions now account for a quarter of all public spending. This is the baby boom and bust.

My mother has gone now, but plenty of her generation are still going strong and, quite understandably, feel justified in drawing their entitlements. After a lifetime of paying in, retirement is their moment for a pay-out. However, because they are such a large generation they are taking out more than they ever put in. The generation born between 1956 and 1961 will take from the welfare state 118 per cent of their contribution. To be a pensioner was once a proxy for being poor and it is a cause for celebration that this is no longer true. The trouble is that we are struggling to pay the bill. The problem is exacerbated by the machinery of politics. Older people vote in greater numbers than younger people and, for that reason, the value of benefits to pensioners has tripled since 1979. Pensioners were deliberately protected, in a way that no other group was, from the consequences of austerity after the financial crash. Politics has become an auction house in which most of the lots appeal to the elderly.

The consequence, unless we settle the question of generational justice, will be a spending crisis of the first order. On current trends, the share of public funds taken by the Departments of Health and Work and Pensions will create an apocalypse for the Department for Communities and Local Government. They will erect the closed sign on the door of the Department for Environment, Food and Rural Affairs. Transport will run slow and Business will not carry on as usual. Britain is facing conflicts that will bear out Pierre Mendès-France's timeless maxim that to govern is to choose. The loving family would always choose to spend the marginal pound on the child in the nursery rather than the grandfather at home. The state, acting *in loco parentis*, chooses to do the opposite. The easiest solution would be for the young to change the political incentives by voting as a phalanx, but that requires a recovery in the esteem of politics which is the seventh question that we shall need to consider.

7 How Do We Restore Faith in Politics?

Politics, as Peel put it, is supposed to supply a sense of popular power and the material outline of a better life. If it has fallen in esteem that is in large part because it has ceased to be reliable in achieving either. Perhaps it is also inevitable, as democracies go through what David Runciman has characterised, in *How Democracies End*, as a 'mid-life crisis', that cynicism becomes habitual. Politicians routinely lie, it is said. Voting changes nothing; they are all in it for themselves. Episodes such as the expenses scandal, or instances of sexual harassment, do as much damage as concrete examples, which are frequent enough, of genuine incompetence.

This is dangerous territory, for the only alternative to established politics is proving to be attractive to many electorates. The trick of the populist is to channel the prejudices, fears and intimations of a section of society. Cast as the tribune of the people, the populist has a ready-made scapegoat in the political class. This is why lazy criticism of the political process is a gift to the enemies of democracy. If the trading and negotiation of politics is not defended then the door is left ajar for unscrupulous politicians. The question has to be not how we replace broken politics with something else but how we recognisably improve it.

There is the rub and there is the nub of the question, because underneath the clichés of cynicism lurks a critique of some merit. The question about the esteem of politics is in fact a question about its efficacy. Britain has stumbled on with an electoral system that no longer produces the executive authority it promises, with moribund political parties financed by interest groups or wealthy individuals, with an upper house of Parliament that is, remarkably for a democracy, not elected and with a civil service that has resisted reform for too long. It is, understandably, difficult to raise much popular interest in and enthusiasm for changes to the constitutional arrangements yet politics, on which we rely to prevent anything worse from rearing its head, cannot be improved without change. And that change, in turn, will not be possible unless we redraw the map of political power in Britain, which is the subject of the eighth urgent question.

8 Where Should Power Lie?

It will take a long time for Britain to recover from its latest argument about the location of sovereign power. The animus of the European referendum and its echo during the departure negotiations will reverberate for at least a generation. Whether or not the economic damage is severe and lasting, the quality of public debate was impaired by a raucous, uncivil and, at times, stupid standard of argument. The deceptively simple injunction to 'take back control' is a demand for a form of sovereignty that no longer exists. The question Britain actually faces is not, as it was posed in the referendum debate, independence or slavery. It is instead, given how much power exists in multinational enterprises and how much has been traded in treaties, how we best pool our sovereignty so that we maintain maximum power for the best effect.

The referendum campaign may have provided a poor answer but it posed a very good question. The impulse for popular control is a noble one and if political life has not been satisfying it, then that needs to be corrected. The implication of the demand for more control is that power has trickled from the hands of the people. There is, indeed, no more centralised developed democracy than Britain. There is no nation in which its provincial towns and cities live deeper in the penumbra of such a shadow cast by its capital. Britain is an unbalanced economy and a concentrated state.

A polity with all its power at the centre no longer works. In 1872 Benjamin Disraeli gave a now celebrated speech in the Free Trade Hall in Manchester in which he set out the public health problems to which government would, and did, supply the answer. When the task is to prevent the spread of contagious disease by the construction of the sewers, then a singular state, with all its purchasing power and command of space, is the ideal means. The public health questions of today involve millions of elderly people treating their own symptoms every day. We have passed from the era of the condition of Britain to the era of the long-term conditions of Britain. The remote state has little relevance to problems like these, and it is little wonder that there has been a sense of lost control.

The decline of deference and an abundance of available information have also changed the relationship of the individual to the state. In all aspects of our lives we are confronted by choices and options, deliberation and decision, but the default setting of the state is still to provide services in bulk order, like it or lump it. The British state runs on an old model of power in which a distant centre does things to people. It is a generation out of date and the consequence is that the services it offers suffer in comparison with the quality of what is available elsewhere. This matters, and not just because public services provide public goods. They also serve to enact a drama of who we are, and this is the penultimate condition of Britain question.

9 How Do We Create an Open Society?

During the tempestuous and uncivil strife of the referendum campaign, Britain did not sound like an open and tolerant nation. The nation is divided along many fissures and it can easily seem as though the chasm between those who have profited from globalisation and those who have been its victims is unbridgeable. This division of values is gradually supplanting economic self-interest as the primary index of electoral allegiance and politicians of the main parties, who have seen their traditional coalitions fracture along these lines, have shown no sign of knowing what to do.

In part the task of leadership is about the renewal of revered British institutions. The most important is the Union of the constituent nations of the United Kingdom, but there are other more surprising elements of a common wealth, such as the monarchy and the Church of England. Action will also be needed to protect the indispensable institution of free speech against the threat it faces from technology – or rather, the threat it faces from uncivil argument conducted too freely on social media platforms. But there is also a task of moral leadership to be undertaken which involves helping to define the sort of nation we wish Britain to be, who is a member of this nation, and what we expect of its citizens. There is no aspect of our life in common in which this form of leadership has failed us more comprehensively than in the argument about immigration. Britain is leaving the EU in large measure because nobody has yet managed to articulate a coherent position on immigration which wins the British people over to the manifest need for this country to remain open to the people of the world.

Britain has a claim to be the most successful multi-cultural experiment on the globe. That does not mean its integration has been perfect – far from it. Indeed there is more we should expect from people of all backgrounds if we are to forge a common life governed by rules adhered to by all. The stringent application of the law is critical for any liberal society. That would then, in turn, permit the most extensive personal freedom in private for worship and style of life. In *The Wealth and Poverty of Nations* David Landes has argued that a liberal and open culture is one of the reasons that Britain became a global force in the first place. To be open and receptive to the world is to be an influence in that world. At a time when the United States of America is led by a President who appears to have no enduring appreciation of diplomatic friendship and when Britain has chosen to abandon its long institu-tional alliance with the various forms of the EU, the ques-tion remains – the final question Britain faces – of what its place in the world should be.

10 What Is Britain's Place in the World?

Britain is a small country that has stood tall in the world. The economic might that was once imperial has been translated into political and diplomatic power. Britain has always been an active participant in world affairs, on rare occasions alone but more usually as a signatory to and presence in international alliances. Through the economic institutions of the Bretton Woods settlement (the World Bank and the International Monetary Fund), NATO, the Security Council of the United Nations and, until recently, the EU, Britain has sat at the top table when the decisions that shaped the post-war world were made. The fear is that this era is coming to a close.

The combination of a more isolationist America and Britain's departure from the EU might conceivably be a disastrous one for a small island just off the European mainland. Already the pressure for the structure of international government to be a better reflection of the shift of economic power to India and China is raising the question of whether Britain's status might be an anomaly. The standard retort has been that Britain translates into European for the Americans and mediates with America for the Europeans. Both sides of that formula are now in jeopardy and Britain is left to contemplate a more modest future. There is, of course, a case for modesty. Britain could decide to retreat to the second rank of nations, attendant princes to the main events. The appetite for British involvement in the troubling problems of the world has receded since the intervention in Iraq. Quietude, masquerading as realpolitik, is a tempting option.

It is a temptation that should be resisted. It is part of remaining open to the world that Britain should in no way retreat. Today's worldwide threats to democracy are severe enough without one of the established democracies voluntarily ceding a position of authority. The case needs to be made to the British people for why it benefits them, as part of a world of pervasive connections, if Britain acts as a moral force for good in world affairs. Of the many things that make Britain the fine nation it is, that concern about the world beyond its own borders is something that we should take pride in.

The Poverty of Philosophy

These ten questions define the condition of Britain today and by the very fact of their having to be asked they arraign the political class for having no viable answers. Though most of the British public do not follow politics in all its intricate detail, the inadequacy of the answers offered has clearly got through. The 2017 general election was a contest that nobody deserved to win, which is why nobody did win. Mrs May asked for a large majority and was rebuffed. Mr Corbyn sought a victory and was denied. It was a stalemate and it holds a lesson that goes beyond a single general election. The old political parties are moribund, perhaps even defunct. The solid social collectives that gave them life have fragmented and dispersed. The axis of politics has tilted; where once parties had firm class foundations, now they do not speak for coherent blocs. Political allegiance is more fluid and volatile but, trapped in their old structures and tribal modes of thought, the main political traditions do not know how to match the times. Silent on the future, the Conservative party and the Labour party are staging a contest to see which of them can most efficiently turn back the clock. The Conservative party is lost in thrall to a fantasy of the utopia before 1973, the mythic year in which Britain lost its identity in the alien embrace of the European project. The Labour party has returned to 1983's attempt to recreate 1974. Beneath these attempts to turn back time lies philosophical poverty. The poor leadership of the two main parties is not a cause of their troubles; it is a consequence, because neither old-time Conservatism nor revivalist Socialism have any answers to the condition of Britain questions.

The political Conservative is hampered by a character-istic lack of ambition. When dramatic change is required, as it is now, it is not wise to look their way in search of it. Indeed, it is not always obvious that a Conservative wants anything much from office beyond the holding of it. Excessive risk-aversion is coupled, in a conservative cast of mind, with a complacent acceptance of the status quo. This amounts, at its worst, to a colossal failure of imagi-nation, the inability to conceive of the world beyond a narrow horizon. Austerity's justification was drily economic; its damage was sadly human. The Conservative understands the fiscal discipline but is less able to widen the enchanted circle to include those affected. The very existence of the doctrine of 'compassionate' Conservatism draws our attention to the fact that compassion is not intrinsic to the creed. It is not true that the Conservative does not care. It is sometimes true that the Conservative does not care *enough*. Instead, the contemporary Conservative has cared excessively about an idea of the nation which bears no relation to the reality of modern sovereignty.

The Labour paradox is that it is a party that talks about a radical future but which is captured by its own past. Labour won its place in British politics after the First World War and its place in British history after the Second. War is a crucible in which endeavour is collective and sacrifices shared. Harold Wilson recorded in his diary that Labour lost the 1951 general election at least in part because the people sniffed that they actually *liked* rationing. Curtailing consumption was the short road to equality. In *The Future of Socialism* Tony Crosland upbraided his party for its joylessness, its hair-shirt tendency. There is a finger-wagging bossiness to Labour politics which knows what is good for you. It is no coincidence that it was Douglas Jay, a Labour economist and politician, who declared that, in matters of food, the man in Whitehall really does know best.

The left is prone to the hunting down of heresies and to doctrinal fighting because it is a textual religion. There is no pantheon of traitors on the political right to match the persistent Labour myth of treachery. Ramsay Macdonald was the first of the type, of which Tony Blair is the most recent, especially in his adventures in foreign policy which have enticed the left into a comfortable fool's position in which all conflict is ultimately traceable to the guilty west. This is the stance of a pressure group rather than a political party which is a serious candidate for office. The Labour party is always more comfortable within its own vintage history than it is in adapting to events. A decade after the 2008 financial crash, Labour still cannot describe how it is possible to conduct social democracy at low cost. Instead, it simply wishes extra money into being for the pleasure of spending it badly.

The modern Tory and the contemporary socialist are both species of conservative and neither can help the nation with its current predicament. Britain faces a battery of pressing questions and the frustrating thing is that answers are at hand. The archive of British political history contains ideas about work, desert, contribution and enterprise that, in modern forms, can guide us through the thicket. Unfortunately neither of the two main parties is drawing on this heritage. Philosophically bereft, they have nothing to say. It is a rare event when both parties turn to face their own dead past at once. The barometer of British politics usually ensures that at least one of the two is able to keep its cool. That is not so today. The chapters that follow point the way to a new destination that we might reach if we summoned the courage to start again.

2

THE COMMON
WEALTH

The Fiscal Philosophers

Limehouse in the old London docks is one of the crucibles of British political life. It was there that, on 30 July 1909, David Lloyd George, Liberal Chancellor of the Exchequer, addressed 4,000 people at the Edinburgh Castle, the former music hall and gin palace that Thomas Barnardo had turned into a coffee house and People's Mission. Lloyd George electrified the crowd with a furious defence of his 'People's Budget', which had introduced taxation on wealth on the grounds that income earned was superior to income unearned. Earned income included wages, salaries and tips. Unearned income in this context referred to capital gains, interest income, passive income generated from rental real estate, stock dividends, and bond interest.

The 1909 budget increased income tax from 1 shilling to 2 shillings in the pound and introduced a 'super-tax' by which anyone who earned over £5,000 a year paid 6d for every pound that their income exceeded £3,000. It also proposed unprecedented taxes on the lands and the unearned incomes of the wealthy. Lloyd George's express intention was to wage a war on squalor and wretched poverty to make it 'as remote to the people of this country as the wolves which once infested its forests'. The most controversial measure in the budget was the proposal for a valuation of all land to be conducted and for a 20 per cent tax to be levied on the increased value of the land when it changed hands.

The protectionist Conservative party, just as it had in the case of Peel and the Corn Laws, sided with the merchant class, preferring instead to place tariffs on imports. The House of Lords also performed its class duty. On 30 November 1909 it rejected the Finance Bill by 350 votes to 75. Asquith, the Prime Minister, dissolved Parliament and the subsequent general election of January 1910 was fought on the issue of the peers versus the people. It was during this campaign that Lloyd George gave his notorious Limehouse speech, which provoked a letter of complaint from the King. The Liberals lost seats in the election but returned to government and the main argument was deemed to have been won. On 28 April 1910 the House of Lords was forced to accept the budget. The turmoil led to the removal of the Lords' power of veto over money bills under the Parliament Act of 1911.

In Limehouse, the Chancellor raised himself to such a pitch of elevation that fiery rhetoric became known thereafter as 'Limehousing'. Lloyd George's act was so popular that he was approached by American theatre producers to perform it on the music hall stage. But the principles he espoused were more than great theatre. Thirteen years later, on 23 November 1922, the MP for Limehouse, who was known for his work with the poor of the area, made his maiden speech in the House of Commons. Clement Attlee spoke passionately about work being a source of dignity superior to welfare and why family was the basic unit of society. Attlee's 1922 Limehouse declaration combined patriotism with passion for the common wealth of the citizens.

In recent times these principles have not been respected. Millions of households have instead faced the prospect of stagnating living standards. On current trends, the average British family will have 15 per cent less cash coming in by 2020 than it had in 2008. At the same time a greater share of GDP is being taken by shareholders as profit. In 1989, for every £1 that GDP grew, the median income grew by 95 pence. By 2007 the family on the median income only got 50 pence from that £1. Until 1990 if you worked harder, you got paid more; now, after you have bought the essentials, you don't.

The introduction of a minimum wage cost no jobs, which shows that companies were paying their staff less than they could afford. In retail and distribution, in which non-unionised workers have no effective power at all, some employers are offering zero-hours contracts, under which they summon labour as and when they need it. How anyone is meant to live like this, let alone thrive, is unfathomable. Britain is creating jobs of a lower status, with lower skills, at lower rates of pay, than any of its competitor nations. It's not an inevitable result of the market economy, because different capitalist nations have different patterns of work. It's a choice and it is one that we could and should avoid. When the top 10 per cent of the population own almost 70 per cent of the wealth, British capitalism has a problem and we need to think again about the principles that we bring to bear on this question. We need to revive the spirit of the common wealth in Britain and, in particular, the three principles on which it should be founded: merit, enterprise and work.

Taxing Questions and Home Truths

These principles need to inform decisions about what to tax. Albert Einstein put the conundrum nicely when he was filling in his tax return: 'This is too difficult for a mathematician. It takes a philosopher'. Choices about what to tax, and at what rate, are leading indicators of a political philosophy. The social democrat tends to see taxation as a way to restore the fairness that goes missing in a market distribution of earnings. It is more than coincidence that the left's favourite self-description, 'progressive', is also the term applied to the regime by which the rich pay a greater proportion in tax than the poor. The conservative is more likely to see tax as a necessary evil.

At current prices and patterns of expenditure, the British state requires £700 billion a year. It has to be raised somehow but taxation in Britain observes no discernible principles at all. This is extraordinary. Taxation is coerced payment; it should be levied according to principles we have chosen to voice and defend. In the common wealth, merit, work and enterprise should be taxed as lightly as possible. Far too much unearned wealth falls, as John Stuart Mill said of the undeserving rich, 'into their mouths as they sleep'. At present in this country, those who have over £1 million of income a year receive a fifth in the form of dividends, interest and property. People with an income between £20,000 and £30,000 receive less than 5 per cent in the same way, and those from the poorest households virtually nothing at all.

We should follow the fiscal principles of the People's Budget: avoid imposts on effort and work; seek, instead, to locate idle wealth and try to place a fiscal deterrent on activity that is evidently harmful to others. The path of least resistance, the easiest way to raise cash, is to tax earnings. But income tax was never meant to be the staple source of revenue. It was introduced in 1798 to raise funds to beat Napoleon and was meant to be temporary. The mandate to levy tax still expires every 5 April, when the government has to reapply for permission with another Finance Act. Yet there is not much chance of the mandate lapsing. Of all the public revenue raised, 44 per cent comes from income tax, a levy on labour which the party of that name is always, strangely, seeking to increase. A further 20 per cent of the tax required comes from business. Consumption taxes account for a further 30 per cent.

The tax base is also heavily reliant – too reliant – on London and on financial services. London is one of only two regions in Britain, the other being the south-east of England, that generates a surplus. During the boom before the financial crash, the rest of the country was subsidised by London and the south-east. London accounts for a quarter of all the income tax paid in the country, which is three times as much as Scotland and more than the north-east, the north-west, Yorkshire and Humberside combined. The capital contributes a quarter of all corporation tax and business rates, and a third of all stamp duty. London and the south-east are bringing in 40 per cent of the total tax take.

Taxation is therefore largely levied on activities that we ought instead to be encouraging – work, creativity and enterprise. We are taxing what is easy to tax rather than what it is right to tax. A meagre 5 per cent of revenue is raised on land and buildings which are static creators of unearned income. The case for taxing land and property, though hardly popular, is clear. Property, unlike income, is hard to hide and taxes on it hard to evade. When domestic residences attract no capital gains tax, property becomes an investment as much as a home. This is a public incentive for the creation of an asset bubble. I am lucky enough to have bought a house yet I cannot meaningfully be credited with earning its rise in value.

Supply in London, where I live, is constrained and, in an open economy, money floods into property in the capital. The lucky ones, like me, enjoy the bonanza while the unlucky, born too late, cannot afford to buy. This makes no sense.

The place to start is the council tax which in England, incredibly, is still based on 1991 house prices. Every house valued at more than £320,000 pays the same amount. Since 1991 the average price of a London house has risen by 399 per cent. In the east Midlands, the region with the lowest house-price inflation in the country, prices have still risen by 219 per cent. At the moment, the owners of a home in the highest band pay three times as much in council tax as the owners of a home in the lowest band even though their home is twenty times the value. Inflate that 1991 figure by the average rise in house prices over the past twenty years, and you get to almost £1 million. The obvious reform is to revalue properties now, and to do so regularly, and to introduce a graded property tax, proportionate to the value of the house. The addition of three new council tax bands could raise £4.7 billion a year. Somebody will always object that they know a little old lady who cannot find a single penny in any one of her twenty-seven rooms, but that's easily dealt with. The debt can be deferred and paid out of the estate.

Higher property taxes would generate revenue from foreign owners who otherwise swerve with ease past the UK tax authorities. If property prices rise the tax take will rise with it. Thus a tax could help to flatten the volatile housing cycle. It would certainly help to redress the gap between the north and the south because 60 per cent of the total revenue on houses worth more than £1 million would be paid by four London boroughs. The whole of England north of, and including, Birmingham would pay only 2 per cent of the total.

If we do not confront the need to tax fairly then there is no hope of solving Britain's housing crisis, which is where the breach of the political covenant is most flagrant. Home ownership, the promise of which has been central to the bargain of British politics, has now fallen to its lowest level since 1987. As land values rise, house building is at its lowest level since 1923. Money is flowing into the existing stock of property from overseas and the planning regime makes new building harder than it should be. A higher divorce rate, later marriage and greater longevity means there are more single-person households than there have ever been. In 1911 only 5 per cent of households contained one person. Now, one in every four houses is occupied by a single person. Since 2008 access to easy mortgage finance has been curtailed. Housing costs for the average family have tripled since 1961, from 6 per cent of income to 18 per cent.

The consequences are even more marked for the younger generations. A generation ago it took the average family three years to save enough for a deposit on a house. Now it would take almost twenty years. The typical age for buying property is moving from the thirties to the forties and there may well be people coming into the labour market now, into clerical and professional jobs, who will never buy a home of their own. The generation of people below the age of thirty spend almost a quarter of their income on housing. That is three times as much as their grandparents spent at the same age.

A government today needs to be judged, as Labour's post-war administration was, on the number of houses that are built on its watch. However, an exclusive focus on ownership is now out of date. The last time the Conservative party really connected with the urban working class was when Margaret Thatcher arranged for 100,000 of them a year to buy the homes once owned by the council. One effect of the sale of the council housing stock, which has been halved since 1981, is that those unable to buy are now thrown on the mercies of private landlords. Half a century ago one in ten thirty-year-olds rented. Now it is four in ten. There are now 11 million people in rented accommodation and, as a sector that has been neglected so long, much of their housing is horribly inadequate.

These are the multiple aspects of a market that simply does not work. At the moment, the high cost of private housing is pushing up rents. The number of rental properties on the market rose 40 per cent in the decade to 2008, but the cost rose 64 per cent. When rental prices soar this high, people go, in turn, to their local authority or to a housing association that passes on 40 per cent of the cost to the taxpayer to pay for housing benefit, the bill for which is rising unsustainably.

Action is needed to revive all three types of tenure. The government needs to build social housing for those who will never earn enough to enter the private market, and that housing then needs to be woven into the city. It was never a good idea to gather all the poorest citizens of a city into large estates such as Becontree in Dagenham or The Wood in Birmingham. Aneurin Bevan entertained the fond hope that these estates would reproduce 'the lovely feature of the English and Welsh village, where the doctor, the grocer, the butcher and the farm labourer all lived in the same street'. In the event, as the better-off first bought their homes and then moved out, and eligibility for new houses became based on need, social housing became housing for poor people.

The private rental market needs to be consolidated. At the moment private rental accommodation is made up of thousands of small suppliers, like plumbing or building, with a single property each. It needs to become much more like retail, with larger professional firms competing to offer a service that runs from cheap but good quality through to premium. The government needs to open up the ground on which we can build. It is sitting on public land that is about twice the size of Leicester. Most of it is in one of three places: London or the respective estates of the NHS and the MoD. It is already the case that 80 per cent of new houses are built on brownfield sites, which is an expensive and dwindling option. It is time to be realistic about the land we need. The artificial boundaries drawn around the cities and designated as greenbelt land need to be redrawn. Only 10 per cent of this country is developed and close on half of that is accounted for by gardens. We have so far built houses on only 1.1 per cent of the land. Sheep and cows have more room to live in than we do. Roads take up only 2.2 per cent of the land, which is less space than reservoirs. There is no danger, either, of interfering with farming, which still enjoys 72 per cent of the British land mass, for the return of a princely 0.5 per cent of British GDP. If we released less than 2 per cent of the available land for housing we could provide homes and gardens for 7 million people.

Even more immovable than buildings is the land on which they stand, a commodity that retains its value, as Mark Twain observed, because they have stopped making it. Land, said Mill, is 'a monopoly not by the act of man but by nature'. There are 60 million acres of land in Britain and much of it is offering an unearned income to its historically fortunate owner. The value of land holdings is clearly parasitic on the labour of others and on public money. It is a part of the common wealth in which all the gains are privately transferred. When the Duke of Westminster's ancestors acquired Mayfair, it was all fields. Now it is packed with development and the land is worth more than £5 billion. This is a windfall gain that derives mostly from public infrastructure and should be taxed as such. So should the gains that accrue from the construction of a high-speed rail link. The economic rent created should be taxed and given to local authorities as an incentive to develop vacant lots. A tax on land discourages property speculation: the asset that lies, literally, underneath the buildings is taxed irrespective of what the developer puts on top of it. There are 600,000 plots of land sitting in land banks, undeveloped, while the nation has a crying need for new housing. A land tax which is not a deterrent to moving like stamp duty, nor regressive like the council tax, would put it to work.

The value of British land is something in the order of £5 trillion. A tax of 2 per cent would raise £100 billion. This is a transformative amount of money. It would allow, if we wished, the abolition of council tax, business rates and stamp duty. It would fund, in addition, a universal entitlement to free, part-time, year-round care for all children aged between two and four years of age. It would pay for social care which needs £3 billion a year and would allow people on low incomes with moderate social care needs to live at home. A further £3 billion could be spent on inserting serious work incentives into the Universal Credit which would mean that, compared with current plans, 340,000 people would evade the poverty trap. Not far short of 5 million people fall into poverty after their excessive housing costs are deducted. The worst-off tenants in the private rental sector spend, on average, a third of their remaining income on rent that is not covered by housing benefit. It would cost £1.2 billion to put this right. The local housing allowance could be reset to ensure that it covered the bottom 30 per cent of local rents and we could pay to build 160,000 new houses every year, half of which would be let at a living rent and half would be offered for shared ownership. The whole package could be funded out of a land value tax.

There is one more unpopular tax which is impossible to justify in a common wealth based on merit, enterprise and work. Of all the levies in the land, inheritance tax is the most loathed and it is easy to understand why. Loving parents do not regard their wealth as theirs alone. They think of the family as a single unit and of children as extensions of themselves. Passing down the heirloom is often part of the incentive for acquiring it in the first place. This is why inheritance tax is feared even though, in 2012, no more than 3 per cent of estates paid it. However, inheritances have doubled over the last two decades. In 2015, £100 billion was passed on and that amount will double again over the next two decades. This is a transfer of wealth and privilege unprecedented in the history of the nation. Yet inheritance tax is very limited. For every £100 raised in taxes nationally only 77p comes from inheritance tax. Compared with the £127 billion of inheritance and gifts, that inheritance tax revenue represents an effective tax rate of only 3.5 per cent. It is also failing to keep pace with the growing importance of wealth transfers. Between 2007 and 2023, inheritance tax receipts are forecast to grow roughly less than a quarter as fast as inheritances. It has become, in effect, a voluntary tax for the rich. A regular above-inflation lifting of the threshold, which started at £100 in 1914, means that inheritance is largely a phantom tax. A levy of 40 per cent begins when an estate is valued at £325,000, unless the recipient is a spouse, a civil partner or a charity. But inheritance is not a virtue, it is just good fortune. The parent has earned the money but the child has not. That is why the bequest should be taxed on receipt. A lifetime receipts tax, paid by the beneficiary, would raise more money than inheritance tax, even with a lower marginal rate. Everyone should have a lifetime receipts tax allowance of £125,000. Beyond that sum, gifts would be taxed at a basic rate of 20 per cent up to £500,000 and at 30 per cent after that. Transfers between spouses could be exempted, as could smaller gifts. The principle of merit permits nothing else and too great an ease of inheritance is, in any case, a blight on creativity and enterprise. There is no chance of a common treasury if we do not respect these principles.

The British left likes to describe the equal society but has always paid too little heed to individual choices. The British right has applauded the free society but with too little understanding of how an unequal distribution of power erodes freedom. The competing visions of the equal society and the free society both embody important values. They come together in *the common wealth*, a term that unearths a buried and wider meaning of wealth; it means a common sense of well-being. The common wealth has a political expression, in the exercise of power in the name of the people. But it is also an economic idea. It is a claim to a share for all in the common treasury of the nation.

Utopia, Limited

I first encountered the idea of common wealth capitalism – not that I would have described it as such at the time – when my father played the role of King Paramount the First, the King of Utopia, in an amateur dramatic society production of Gilbert and Sullivan's *Utopia, Limited* in Bolton, Lancashire. The sub-title of *Utopia, Limited* is *The Flowers of Progress*, which is a good description of the claim capitalism makes for itself.

Arthur Sullivan's book was based, improbable as it may seem, on the Companies Act of 1862 which he refers to, incorrectly, in the lyrics as the Joint Stock Companies Act, probably echoing the 1844 Act, which had featured in *The Gondoliers*. Is there a more unlikely refrain in musical theatre than: 'All hail, astonishing Fact!/All hail, Invention new/The Joint Stock Company's Act/The Act of Sixty Two'. But it really was a great invention new. The combined effect of the 1844 Act, Edward Pleydell-Bouverie's 1855 Limited Liability Act and Robert Lowe's Companies Act of 1862 was to create the greatest engine of prosperity in human history: the modern corporate enterprise.

The man behind the Act, the man commemorated though not named by King Paramount the First, was one of my predecessors as an editorial writer on *The Times*. After a spell in politics in Australia, Robert Lowe had returned to Britain in 1850 where he joined *The Times*.

Lowe then went back into politics and rose, under Gladstone, to be the President of the Board of Trade and, eventually, Chancellor of the Exchequer. Lowe is not a renowned figure in British political life, but he ought to be because he did more than any single figure to bring modern capitalism into being and to define the public limited company. And there, in that description, is the critical point. It is the *public* limited company, operating according to public virtue, as a contribution to the common wealth. The objective of Lowe's Act was to remove vexatious legal restrictions on companies of seven or more members. Unlimited liability, he told Parliament in February 1856, was 'the Corn Law of the capitalist'. The Act permitted a company to be created as a separate legal entity, like a person in its own right. This had the effect of limiting the liability of shareholders to the investment they had offered, rather than the whole debt of the company.

It was a privilege that came to be exploited. After the rehearsal rooms of *Utopia, Limited*, my next acquaint-ance with capitalism was on 3 May 1997, on the trading floor of an investment bank. My first day as an equity strategist at HSBC James Capel was the day that Gordon Brown gave operational independence to the Bank of England. My job, advising managers of money where to allocate their capital, was a five-year schooling in the assumption that shareholders must be the kings para-mount. Under pressure for instant returns, companies were forced to act as if their life cycle were measured in months rather than years. A damaging connection, stripped of all desert, was established between failure and payment. Mergers and acquisitions were preferred to organic growth; business ethics gave way to rent-seeking. Corporate fraud and malfeasance subsequently corroded trust and so did tax evasion. The vital sense of a company existing through time was lost. Desert went missing from the corporate enterprise.

Years later, I found myself comparing that experience with the original corporate template when I followed Lowe and became a leader writer on *The Times*. The first editorial I wrote was about the fall of Lehman Brothers in November 2008, and the decision of Hank Paulson, US Treasury Secretary, to use public funds to prevent a collapse of the banking system. My editorial was a reflection, when the complexity of financial instruments had far exceeded the wisdom of regulators, on the privatisation of gain and the nationalisation of loss. The consequences of that day ramify into our politics still. A decade on, growth has barely recovered and populist politics has flourished in its absence. It was easy enough to observe and even easier to write a stiff editorial in *The Times*. It was a lot harder to know what to do.

The answer lies in going back to Lowe. The good name of capitalism fell alongside the banks in 2008 but the best response to bad capitalism has to be better capitalism. This better nature can be found in its origins. Unfortunately, we have travelled a long way from the founding idea. In the twenty-first century too many companies answer the description Ambrose Bierce gave to the corporation during the Gilded Age of American business: 'an ingenious device for obtaining individual profit without individual responsibility'.

The idea of the capitalist enterprise, floating free of public obligation beyond a commitment to work within the law, is nonsensical. A company is given the ability to govern itself through by-laws of its own choosing, the capacity to buy and sell property and to sue and be sued in its own name, by a political act expressed in a body of law. Limited liability means that the joint stock company is underwritten by a process of public reasoning. A complex series of laws and torts regulate the way that individuals and corporations can behave. This is not a body without obligations – an idea for which there is no foundation either in law or in history.

When the idea of an association endowed with a collective identity was pioneered by Roman jurists two millennia ago, it was licensed by the state expressly to further *public* purposes. Into the eighteenth and nineteenth centuries, English and American lawyers used the precedents and vocabulary of Roman civil law in describing and defining corporations. At the time the only way that private capital could be induced to take such a risk was if the venture was given the award of a royal charter, like the East India Company, the Hudson's Bay Company and the Virginia Company. It is little wonder that Sir William Blackstone, the great eighteenth-century English jurist and author of the definitive textbook of the English common law, referred to corporations as 'little republics'. The corporation was the means by which a state could channel private capital to achieve public ends such as the building of a bridge, a turnpike or a canal. In America, a country that did not have a wealthy aristocracy, John Quincy Adams spoke for many when he described the joint stock company as a 'truly republican institution' that allowed investment by 'the poor ... females and children ... the widow and the orphan'. The lack of a public purpose was thought to be sufficient grounds for denying a corporate charter and the failure to fulfil public responsibilities was enough to get a charter revoked.

There are some obvious requirements of good companies. The most basic is that they should pay their dues in taxation. It is possible to offend a social norm while breaking no law and plenty of companies are doing so. Nine out of ten British people think tax avoidance is wrong and they are right to think there is a problem. Six of the top ten multinational companies in Britain paid no UK corporation tax in 2014 despite posting profits globally between them of more than £30 billion. In 2016, on a revenue of £1 billion, Google paid just £36.4 million in tax. Caffe Nero has 613 shops in the UK and Ireland which, since 2007, have generated more than £1 billion in sales. They have paid not a penny in corporation tax. Think of the book you are holding in your hands. The bookshop you bought it from will have paid a rate of taxation that is eleven times what Amazon pays. In 2016 Amazon paid just £7.4 million in tax on turnover of £1.5

billion. No doubt it is possible to allocate costs so that profitability is hidden and taxes are avoided, but everybody knows what they are doing.

Companies need to be good employers but we also need to attend to the 5 million people in Britain who are now self-employed. Self-employment has accounted for almost half of employment growth since May 2008. The gig economy can be split between those in privileged and those in precarious positions. The privileged find flexibility their ally. It allows them to work for themselves, or at their own convenience, or to take a greater share of the return on their labour. The precarious are self-employed because their other options, when they exist, are less advantageous. Forty per cent of self-employed jobs are in the privileged category and 60 per cent are defined as precarious. They can be found in joinery and plumbing, construction, education, retail, cleaning, taxis and hairdressing. It has become too cheap and too easy for companies to raise productivity by adding a worker on a low wage rather than by investing in new technology or new methods. The self-employed are more likely than the employed to work less than they would like. The precarious group of the self-employed are also more likely to be young, less likely than employees to be given any training or to benefit from a single-tier pension. In the common wealth, statutory maternity pay should be extended to the self-employed at a rate of 90 per cent of earnings for the first six weeks.

Workers need good representation which they are not getting. The revival of effective trade unions will be a priority in the common wealth. Trade unions were once the largest voluntary associations in the land, the big platoons of civil society. Trade union negotiation has the 40-hour week, the right to paid holiday, legal rights of contract for employees and the creation of the weekend on its roster of achievements. Not so much now, though. Membership of trade unions has declined from a peak of fourteen million in 1979 to six million today and most of that is in declining industries or the public sector. When Britain is the European capital of fragile work too many people are going unspoken for. In the common wealth there will be incentives for entrepreneurs to establish new challenger trade unions which will offer a range of services to members that include negotiation at work, financial help in the manner of the friendly societies and brokering any complex interactions with public agencies.

The Open Economy

A vigorous defence of the recast corporate enterprise needs to be accompanied by an equally adamant case for the virtues of an open market economy. As Robert Lowe said in Parliament in defence of his Act:

Who could have imagined it possible that a state of society resting on the most unlimited and unfettered liberty of action, where everything may be supposed to be subject to free will and arbitrary discretion, would tend more to the prosperity and happiness of man than the most matured decrees of senates and of States? These are the wonders of the science of political economy, and we should do well to profit by the lesson, which that science has taught.

The common wealth will be founded on ethical companies in an open economy. Where the market economy spills out inequalities, they need to be tamed and dealt with. Too unequal a society is a blight and calls into question the very order that created it. By the same token, the wealth has to be created in order for the question of distribution even to arise. But that does not mean we should fall for the false and easy promises of protectionism. Free trade was once the cause of the radicals and should become so again. Manchester became renowned, in Disraeli's phrase, as 'the philosophical capital of the world' precisely because of the assault on the establishment that it mounted in the name of free trade. The men who won the abolition of tariffs on corn knew that there was no quicker way to impoverish ourselves than to yield to the myth that tariff walls will protect our incomes. Ronald Reagan once described protectionism as destructionism because its victims are the poor. It is a point the current Republican holder of the Presidency would do well to note.

The temptation of economic nationalism is perennial. Most countries have histories of tariff protectionism, as the development economist Ha-Joon Chang showed in his book *Kicking Away the Ladder*. However, since the end of the Second World War, a series of international agreements, such as the General Agreement on Tariffs and Trade, have helped to foster freer trade. There are, to this day, many extant levies. The US protects its steel industry. The worst part of the EU is the vast subsidy to agricultural producers. India has by no means fully unwound its complex array of tariffs and China does not exactly respect the conventions of free trade. There are today thirty-seven countries that apply tariff rates in double digits.

This is in defiance of what we know about the benefits. Adam Smith attributed the flourishing of Egypt, Greece, Rome, Bengal and China to their trading. Over the past thirty years the economies that grew fastest have been those that traded the most. Trade produces substantial aggregate gains measured both in wages and the range of available goods. The 2016 Index of Economic Freedom confirms that citizens of countries that embrace free trade are better off than those in countries that do not. Trade has brought higher incomes to millions of people in China and in India, in the largest surge from poverty in all of human history. Much of the purpose of trade is to be an antidote to poverty.

This will only be true if, in the economy of the common wealth, concentrated power is broken up. The strategy for tackling companies that are too big comes from the same decade as the distinction between earned and unearned income. The twenty-sixth and twenty-seventh Presidents of the United States, Theodore Roosevelt and William Taft, pioneered an approach to capitalism that we should emulate. Adam Smith pointed out the conspiracies that businessmen, when they gather, tend to practise against the public. Marx pointed out capitalism's inexorable tendency towards monopoly. Roosevelt and Taft were conscious of both problems and so were, for that reason, fine friends of capitalism. They were operating, much as we are now, during an epochal shift. The agricultural economy of the United States, which had been torn in two by the Civil War, had been transformed into a great industrial power. However, a stock market crash in 1893 had caused a depression that squeezed middle-class incomes. Roosevelt concluded that this was due to a structural flaw rather than a cyclical inevitability. The exclusion of ordinary folk, he decided, was in the nature of American capitalism. The problem with the 'trusts', to use the term of the time, was that they concentrated power in private hands to the detriment of the common wealth. 'Liberty produces wealth and wealth destroys liberty' wrote Henry Demarest Lloyd in *Wealth Against Commonwealth*, an influential indictment of the trusts published in 1894. The President made the case for the power of state attorney to step in to force real competition on the reluctant capitalists. Hence the prosecutions for market fixing (forty-five by Roosevelt and seventy-five by Taft) that were brought under the Sherman Antitrust Act of 1890. Hence the enforced break-up, in 1911, of

Rockefeller's behemoth Standard Oil, which owned 88 per cent of refined oil flows in America.

Corporate power is once again a serious concern. Before the crash of 2008, banking was dominated by companies that, in a network of invisible technological alliances, were too big to fail, for fear of the consequences. But the principle of the public interest must mean that there can be nothing sacrosanct about any given corporate setting, even where it has grown large simply through clever enterprise. Congealed corporate power corrodes the common wealth just as much as accumulated political power. A Bain study of 315 global corporations found that just one or two players in each market earned, on average, 80 per cent of the economic profit. Market power of this kind allows dominant firms to set their own prices. There are plenty of markets in the UK which are so concentrated. *The Economist* recently calculated that more than half of the 250 industries they assessed had become more concentrated over the last decade, which meant that the four biggest firms accounted for a greater share of the revenue.

Broadband, telecommunications, mobile telephony and personal current accounts are all examples but the most conspicuous are the technology companies. Google has more than a 90 per cent share of general search in most European countries. YouTube has a 56 per cent share worldwide of its market; Amazon a 95 per cent share of the market for e-books; Facebook a 61 per cent share of social media. These near-monopoly positions are, unaccountably, helped by legal exemptions. Facebook and Google are rarely held responsible for what users do on them, unlike publishers. We urgently need new rules to deal with data just as new rules were once drafted to deal with intellectual property. The technology companies are harvesting valuable data on the behaviour and habits of their clients. We need to devise rules that give individuals rights to their data. Markets, without regulatory devices, produce giants which then refuse to operate by the rules of the markets. The most successful competitors bring an end to competition. That is their express aim and, in the name of the common wealth, they need to be prevented. Capitalists may not like competition but capitalism without it is just private power. In the common wealth all companies will be put on notice.

I, Robot

That must apply most notably to the technology companies, the corporate giants of our time, who have found the secret of generating revenue without people. Apple makes $2.1 million of revenue for every employee; Facebook makes $1.4 million. The equivalent figure for an employee at Procter and Gamble is $0.7 million. Technology has, for centuries, abetted the march of progress. The fear now is that technology has become the enemy of the common wealth. The fear runs very deep, all the way down to the anxiety that labour is on the cusp of becoming obsolete. The robots – Karel Čapek's word, which is the Slavic for labour, from his 1920 play *Rossum's Universal Robots* – are going to take over and, once they have colonised work, they may well sweep through the nation murdering the needless humans in a fit of programmed logic.

Since the invention of the integrated circuit in 1958, computing power has doubled twenty-seven times. Previous waves of technological innovation attacked industries one by one which meant that the economy could diversify and see off the threat. The next revolution in information technology could be different as it attacks almost all industries at the same time. Any employee whose work is at all predictable is now coming within the sight of the robots. The first decade of the twenty-first century, in the US and UK, has passed with the net creation of no new jobs. Opportunities in novel industries, such as computing, are not keeping pace with the destruction in employment caused by the same. A recent report by Deloitte suggested that, within two decades, 60 per cent of today's jobs in retail could be automated. Almost three-quarters of the jobs in transport could easily be done by simple machines or complex robots, and automation in factories, already extensive, will continue apace. The pessimists say the robots are coming and the resultant loss of employment will so drastically erode the tax base of the modern state, not to mention deprive whole populations of meaningful work, that a catastrophe looms on the horizon. Machinery does the labour with great efficiency. No robot will ever call in sick or go on strike or get tired or waste time chatting. Productivity will rise but all the rewards will go to the owners of capital. Advanced societies, and here China will rapidly figure, will be home to a squalid class of the destitute, a middle class dependent on philanthropy and a wildly wealthy plutocracy.

And then it gets worse. In the phase of technological development that follows, algorithms will move beyond processing into perception. The point at which artificial intelligence passes the cognitive capacity of the brain is known as 'the singularity'. Peak horse power arrived at the end of the twentieth century; peak human power might be on the threshold now. The threat might even extend to writers. An algorithm called Alice (Artificial Linguistic Internet Computer Entity) promises to master diction and script. She already has the visual sophistication to select and stack boxes. The next frontier, a simulation of reflective intelligence, promises mass unemployment. Robots are useful in, for example, manufacturing, assembly, packing and packaging, Earth and space exploration, surgery, weaponry, laboratory research and the mass production of consumer goods. The more sophisticated the merger between computing capacity and vast archives of data, the greater the likelihood that robots will go on to perform jobs as varied as radiology in hospitals, refurbishing stock in supermarkets, driving planes, trains and automobiles, defusing bombs and serving drinks in bars. In economies based on consumer spending, mass unemployment promises the end of days. That's not all, though. Robots are now flying, swimming, sailing, driving cars and going away for the weekend together.

However, there is really no need to capitulate to misery. Every industrial revolution is a dance between displacement and compensation and there are reasons to suppose that we can cope. Since 1750, successive labour-saving technologies have boosted productivity by an average of 1.1 per cent a year, which means that the economy grows by a third every generation. Every industrial revolution changes the nature of work. In 1700 agriculture accounted for half of all employment. After the era of the spinning jenny and the steam engine, employment on the land declined, to the point where just one in a hundred workers is employed there today. Mass industrialisation in the second half of the nineteenth century meant that, by 1900, manufacturing accounted for 45 per cent of all jobs. Today, after a revolution in information technology shrank the world and reduced its costs, only 10 per cent of British workers are in manufacturing. Work in the service sector has doubled in every century since 1700, to the point where services now provide 80 per cent of all employment. However, though work has changed in type, its quantity has been unaffected by technological development and so have its rewards. Since 1750, wages have risen by an average of 0.9 per cent a year, much the same as the rise in productivity. Educational attainment made workers more valuable, which tamed income inequalities. Work passed from hand to brain but not to the ghosts in the machines.

The discussion about artificial intelligence is like a replay of the argument between Condorcet and Malthus about population in the last decade of the eighteenth century. Malthus thought that population growth heralded inevitable catastrophe. Condorcet thought societies would adapt. Ingenuity can defeat fatalism again. For all its ability with numbers, the supercomputer is, as Steven Pinker points out in *How the Mind Works*, about equal to the nervous system of a snail. Computers struggle to mimic the intuitive creativity that comes naturally to human beings. A computer has no trouble remembering a twenty-five digit number but will struggle to recall the basic gist of *Little Red Riding Hood*. In 2012, it took 16,000 computers frantically mimicking brain activity to recognise a cat. I have known some pretty stupid people in my time but almost none of them would have any trouble recognising a cat. In a word, robots struggle to do what humans are adept at; they struggle to adapt. The independent mechanical spirits of Isaac Asimov's *I, Robot* remain a science fiction fantasy.

Automation is, of course, a threat to some jobs but new options will be abundant too. Healthcare, energy and transportation are evolving into information industries. Smartphones and wearable devices will make healthcare delivery and data collection more effective and personal, while computational bioscience and customised molecular medicine will radically improve drug discovery and effectiveness. Artificial intelligence will assist doctors, and robots will increasingly be used for surgery and care for the elderly. We will, in some way, become more productive than we were precisely because automation accelerates routine processes. Incomes will grow and demands for new products will arise. The ingenuity of human behaviour will be roused in the face of change, as it always is. New tastes will be formed and new work created. The robots can do the most unpleasant jobs but there will be plenty of tasks, such as serving in restaurants, which are capable of being automated but which will still be performed by human beings because that is what people want. Even if the tireless robots do all the work, that only shifts the political question from the creation to the distribution of the rewards. Robots may take jobs but they add to prosperity. Robots, like all machines only more so, blur the line between capital and labour. This is capital that does the labour.

This merger between capital and labour will, if we do not act, represent another shift of power towards shareholders. To avoid this, compulsory profit sharing could be introduced into firms above a certain size. In France, profit sharing has been mandatory since the 1960s for firms with more than fifty employees. The profits shared are exempt from employers' national insurance contributions and employees' income tax. Employee Ownership Trusts (EOTs) would strengthen the stake that workers hold on the value they create. The Trust is a form of collective ownership which has a controlling interest in the company and which distributes shareholdings to individual employees in the form of cash bonuses tax-free up to £3,600 per annum. If the robots are making all the money, then I need to be the proud owner of an Alice who writes my next book as I enjoy the wealth and fame she produces on my behalf. If popular capitalism is not the best response to automation, then we could establish a Citizens' Wealth Fund. This would be a portfolio of assets, publicly owned but managed independently of government, which paid a universal capital dividend. The whole nation would then share the fruits of productivity improvements. The Fund could be capitalised initially through a mix of capital receipts transfers, asset sales and dedicated wealth taxes raised for the purpose. It would be a pleasing irony if, as the public stakes in the investment banks were gradually realised, the proceeds were used to capitalise a Citizens' Wealth Fund. If a similar fund had been created from the North Sea oil revenues, it would be worth over £500 billion today.

Common Wealth Capitalism

This matters enormously because capitalism, properly organised and regulated, remains the shortest road to the common wealth. In the eight hundred years before 1820, income per head across the world was static and so was life expectancy. Life wasn't much more than a matter of choosing which noxious disease to die from. In the two hundred years of industrial capitalism, income per head has risen by 800 per cent. Life expectancy has tripled.

These are among the achievements of common wealth capitalism, which was a moral question from the start. In *The Protestant Ethic and the Spirit of Capitalism*, Max Weber pointed out that thrift and providence, the Christian virtues, were the perfect grounding for the pursuit of profit. Markets were never 'free'; they were always regulated by a moral sense.

The principles of merit, enterprise and work must endure. At the moment they are not being respected and the point at which this bites hardest is pay. Adam Smith once wrote that the symbol of decency for the labourer was that he should have a linen shirt to go to work in. To have to work bare-chested was an exhibition of poverty that added a social insult to the injury of penury. Each year now the Joseph Rowntree Foundation (JRF) works out the equivalent of a linen shirt today. Their assessment of the income people require to live a reasonable life is the set of goods of which it feels wrong to be deprived as a member of a moral community. The JRF list is drawn up by a panel of citizens who have concluded that a decent life demands a great deal more than food and shelter. The modern linen shirt is a holiday in the UK, a telephone and the occasional meal out.

It is possible, of course, to stay alive without these items but it is not possible to be a member of the common wealth and that – rather than mere survival – should be the aim in a wealthy democracy. The cost of a decent moral life in Britain, defined by the jury of citizens at the JRF, is £17,000 for a single person and £39,000 for a working couple with two children. That implies an hourly wage of £8.62 for the single person and £9.91 for each of the couple. The national living wage is currently £7.83 an hour, which leaves the single person £4,000 short of the target sum and the couple £13,000 short. This is a more generous interpretation of what we need to be an active citizen in the common wealth than the poverty line, which is set at just under £9,000 per annum, a line under which one in every four British adults and children already falls. There is no reason why, in a prosperous country, children should be raised in poor households and the solution is on the title page of the annual Joseph Rowntree Foundation report. The clue is in the name of the organisation.

As a child Joseph Rowntree was deeply affected by a visit he made to Ireland during the 1845 potato famine. As we now know, famines are not about the lack of food. They are about the lack of entitlement to food, which is to say the lack of income. The young Rowntree resolved there and then to look after his employees properly. When he opened his chocolate factory in York in 1869, Rowntree established good pay, housing benefits and the first occupational pension scheme for his workers. The Rowntrees looked after the company and that meant looking after the people in it.

Welfare is the bill that falls on the public realm when the private realm fails in its duty to its workers. Not every company can afford to pay its employees more, but many could without losing jobs as a result. The national living wage should rise every year in an increment just above the rate of inflation until it does what its title purports to do. In the common wealth, the gap between the value of work and the cost of a decent life needs to close to nothing. The human race is the only species whose needs change across time and space. The workers of York needed one set of goods in 1869 and quite another in 2018. One thing, however, remains the same. The answer to a decent life can be found in a return to the republican origins of the company, in a reformed capitalism that treats its workers as the producers of national prosperity rather than as chattels prospecting wealth for shareholders. The answer is in the story of Joseph and the Chocolate Factory.

When five families in Britain own more than the poorest 12 million citizens, that erodes, as the Bank of England governor Mark Carney has said, the social capital on which the system depends. The common wealth is an idea of justice applied to the production of wealth. There are many competing notions of justice but the most compelling among them rest on a conception of merit. We need to deserve what we get and when we receive something for which there was no warrant we feel a sharp sense of unfairness. This feeling, justice as what is due, is a deep popular instinct which has not been respected by the political parties.

The British left has an egalitarian notion which consists of reducing the gap between the richest and the poorest. In the left's idea of justice it does not matter much how the pattern of income distribution is arrived at as long as the gaps between people are deemed to be the right size. The British right commits the exact opposite error. When it is not disparaging the very idea of trying to find a just settlement in politics, politicians of the right tend to suppose that any reward legally arrived at must *ipso facto* be just. Neither of these two ideas will do. The common wealth must be richer, in every sense. It will never quite be Utopia, Limited; no open society ever is. But it will be the next chapter in the tale by which British politics honours and serves its people rather than neglects them.

3

THE LIBERAL
DEMOCRACY

The Silent Ballot

The fleet of cars moved uncommonly slowly in procession, as if in a funeral cortège, past the statue of Peel by Bury Parish Church. But this was not a funeral; it was a celebration. For those who applauded the election, on 1 May 1997, of a Labour government, after eighteen years of the Conservatives in office, it was already clear that this was going to be a triumphant night, but that was not the thought that struck me as the cars passed sedately through the near-deserted streets. It felt more elevated than that and more important. I was witnessing a beautiful democratic ritual in which the ballot boxes were brought from the polling stations all over town for volunteers to count the the vote.

I was taken aback to be close to tears at the silent and civilised transfer of power. The result, when it was entered in the early hours, would confirm the status of Bury North as a political barometer. The town that always chose the winner had done so again. David Chaytor was returned as Bury's first Labour MP since 1979. But above and before that was the ritual of democracy itself. Gently, graciously and with no injury inflicted, the Conservatives left office and Labour took power. It is a common enough thought that the ballot box is preferable to the barrel of a gun but it is no less important for being familiar.

In the maelstrom of our unpleasant politics and uncivil argument, it can be hard to make the case for the nobility of public life. It will continue to be hard until politics once again provides the people with a sense of agency and the feasible prospect of a higher quality of life. The realisation of those virtues depends, in turn, on two components of a viable polity. The first is that we need to revive the reputation of politics. A descent into cynicism hurts us all. A vicious conversation loudly amplified across ungoverned social media platforms will make a life in common impossible.

The second is that politics will need to be recast if it is once again to produce the results that citizens have a right to expect. British political institutions have ceased to do their duty. Power is in all the wrong places and the functions of government do not redound to the greater benefit of the citizen body. When we bother to elect them at all, the way we elect our representatives is broken. It can be hard to see the direct connection between the workings of the state and the daily grind of our lives. Yet popular sovereignty is worthless if government delivers no benefits. The cars gently rolling through the streets to bring the ballot boxes to the verdict really do embody a beautiful idea. We need politics to be better so that it can be worthy of the silent hopes invested in that moment.

In Defence of Politics

In the town hall in Siena in Italy hangs a fourteenth-century fresco which defines the questions at stake. Ambrogio Lorenzetti's *Allegory of Good and Bad Government* makes three claims for politics: that government affects human lives; that we can distinguish good government from bad; and that we therefore have a moral choice before us. Fifty years ago Bernard Crick wrote a book called *In Defence of Politics* in which he asserted the virtues of politics against a range of foes that included ideology, nationalism, technology and false friends. All of those are still active dangers, but to them we need to add the corrosive effect of cynicism.

The popular view of politics today is best caught by Harold Macmillan's joke that the collective noun for heads of government is 'a Lack of Principals'. Perhaps trust in politics *was* higher in Macmillan's time than it is now but trust in all institutions was higher in a more deferential, less scrutinised age. It is not likely that Winston Churchill would have been so trusted if his drinking and messy financial affairs had been held up to the light. Britain's most trusted man is Sir David Attenborough, but I doubt his reputation would endure if he were put in charge of building a third runway at Heathrow Airport. At least some of this decline in trust is a direct consequence of a salutary refusal to take one's elders and betters at their own estimation. Politics is not, in any case, a vocation likely to inculcate trust. It is unpredictable and adversarial and change works to a slower timetable than the patience of the electorate. Nasty events turn up unannounced and your political allies, let alone your enemies, lay snares for the unwary. It is an arena in which partial views clash; there is no room for the disinterested.

Democratic reasons why trust in politics might be low are welcome but we need to avoid various terrible arguments for a lack of faith. There are three overlapping accusations about politics that need to be countered. They are the claims that politicians are free of genuine convictions and only in it for themselves; that they lie and cheat; and that the whole system is corrupt.

There are scoundrels in politics, of course, and there always have been. They exist in every party but they are not, in truth, very numerous. The cardinal problem of British politics is not that it is staffed by knaves, and it would be foolish to permit 'Westminster' to function in British political language in the way that 'Washington DC' can be made to do in the American idiom, as a signifier of an elite conspiracy against the people. It is, in fact, a rare politician that does not begin with a set of convictions, however inchoate and however inadequate they prove to be when they collide with reality. Things constantly go awry but rarely because evil politicians are cunningly carrying out their plan of self-enrichment. It is more usually because they disagree or because their competence fails them. Conspiracies in politics are rare; chaos is permanent. We are charging the politicians with two contradictory accusations: that they are so fiendishly clever that they can secretly organise public resources for their own benefit and, at the same time, they are completely useless.

The assumption of bad faith leads directly on to the stronger accusation that political lying is endemic. I once found myself on a radio programme, listening down the line to a long and rambling answer by the psychologist Oliver James in response to a question about Barack Obama and the importance of hope in politics. Mr James had veered off the topic because he was determined to allege that Tony Blair had lied over the Iraq war. He concluded his monologue with what I regarded as the fantastic claim that 'one in two people in this country is on the verge of mental illness.' To which I replied: 'Well, that's certainly true in this conversation.' I maintained that to call someone a liar is not an accusation that should be levelled lightly.

We have to bear in mind that the price for telling a political lie is, rightly, very high. Lies that hide corrupt intent and practice need to be exposed and their practitioners shamed. The man whose name was ticked in the boxes I saw heading to the count on 1 May 1997 is a sad case in point. David Chaytor was elected to Parliament as the MP for Bury North. His maiden speech, on 17 June that year, was a paean to Sir Robert Peel. Mr Chaytor became a diligent MP and a strong advocate of state education and green issues from the Labour back benches. In May 2009 he referred himself to the Parliamentary Commissioner for Standards for claiming £13,000 in mortgage expenses on a home on which the mortgage had already been paid. In February 2010 it was announced that Mr Chaytor would be charged under the Theft Act 1968 relating to false accounting. In December of that year he pleaded guilty to that charge and was sentenced to eighteen months in prison. His appeal for leniency regarding the severity of the sentence was refused and the Lord Chief Justice described his behaviour as 'calculating', involving 'the careful preparation of bogus claims'. In the event, he served five months in prison under the terms of home detention curfew.

Every one of the MPs who were either sanctioned by the parliamentary officials or who served a prison term deserved their punishment. Politicians like Mr Chaytor who betray their own trade are polluting the very air they breathe. Yet it would be a shame if their cases became parables of the declining trust in politicians in Britain. Being a good politician is harder than it looks. The difficulty of the task goes further towards explaining the fact that so few people are good at it than does the accusation that people attracted to politics must be venal and self-serving. Ultimately, trust in politics rests on the power it grants and the results it produces. British institutions have grown old and they are creaking. The structure of power in the common wealth needs urgent attention.

Sovereign Power

The paramount question to answer in any political state is: Where does power lie? The strict definition of a sovereign power is that it accords the full right and power of a governing body over itself. In this account of power, sovereignty is conceived of as absolute and perpetual. All must gather, argued Thomas Hobbes in *Leviathan*, in the commonwealth (his word). There they must submit to the sovereign power who would compel the dissolute to act for the common good which was inalienable, indivisible and infallible. There has been more than a distant echo of this in the debate about Britain's departure from the EU. There is a branch of thought, which has taken root in the Conservative party, that locates sovereign power, indivisible and absolute, in Parliament. For those who take this view, entangling British laws into European institutions always meant the loss of sovereign power, the loss, in other words, of democratic virtue.

This argument is a disguised form of nationalism rather than a demand for democracy per se. The EU, it is true, is a long way from an ideal of democratic accountability and its critics often make this point. Too much of what it does originates in the unelected Commission; the

Council of Ministers is a poor regulator of the Union's bureaucratic ingenuity and the European Parliament has a tendency to meddle but little authority to act. I would echo all of this myself and if Britain were at any point to wish to rejoin the EU this democratic deficit would have to have been met. Yet the prominent advocates of Brexit are not interested in a more democratic Europe. Their real criticism stems from the credo that sovereign power belongs at the level of the nation-state. Indeed, they are actively opposed to more democratic institutions in the EU because they fear conferring legitimacy in the wrong place. For them, Britain should be the indivisible sovereign power.

There is nothing necessarily ignoble about this idea; it is simply impossible to reconcile with the complexities of modern states. Sovereignty today cannot feasibly be absolute, perpetual and indivisible. In a world shrunk by instant communication this purist, pre-modern conception of sovereignty makes as much sense as phrenology. Regulations cross boundaries to enable markets to work smoothly. Companies operate in many nations at once. Countries are voluntarily enmeshed in systems of international law. The very idea of a treaty, such as NATO for example, involves the concession of absolute power, accorded in order that power may grow and security may be enhanced. Jurisdiction is often disputed between rival courts of law, either in a federated state or between nation-states in supra-national judicial institutions such as the European Court of Justice. Many of the issues for which the state retains responsibility – crime, climate change, immigration – cannot possibly be addressed at the level of the nation.

The idea of a single nation taking back control is a chimera. Sovereignty, in modern states, is either divisible or it is meaningless. You would have thought that the people most likely to understand the idea of sharing sovereignty would be the British. The Act of Union of 1707 created the unitary state now known as the United Kingdom by sharing sovereignty among constituent nations. The systems of currency, taxation and law were all brought together but some features of governance, notably religion and education, remained separate. In Britain we have lived and thrived in a state that pools sovereignty. The Act of Union is one of the nation's great political achievements which, as long as the consent of the peoples remains, should stay in place. The notion that shared sovereignty applies within Britain but not beyond its borders is an obsolete form of self-harm. Alas, that harm has been done and Britain is leaving the comity of European nations. All the more reason, then, for getting the state in order.

The Lowest Level

It is a beautiful irony that the principle to guide us in the location of power comes from within the EU. The idea of subsidiarity was borrowed from Alexis de Tocqueville and embodied in Protocol 2 of the Maastricht treaty. In *Democracy In America*, de Tocqueville wrote that 'decentralisation has not only an administrative value but also a civic dimension, since it increases the opportunities for citizens to take interest in public affairs; it makes them get accustomed to using freedom. And from the accumulation of these local, active, persnickety freedoms, is born the most efficient counterweight against the claims of the central government.'

Subsidiarity is the unlovely word, in the pickled Euro-jargon, for this elegant idea. It means that social and political issues should be dealt with at the lowest viable level. Whereas the idea of devolution implies that power rests rightfully at the centre until it is pushed downwards, the implication of subsidiarity is that power belongs with the individual. Where people have the information to make their own choices they retain the power to do so. This power can encompass holding the budget for your own social care, choosing a school for your child or a hospital and a doctor for your operation.

However, this does not mean that individuals will want to assume the burden of running complex services. Oscar Wilde pointed out that socialism would never happen because there aren't enough evenings in the week. Tony Crosland meant much the same thing when he objected to industrial democracy on the grounds that people would rather be at home doing their gardening. Though we should be delighted at their active citizenship when groups of parents do want to establish a free school in their locale, most will not. Most services will require, in practice, public and collective provision. However, the principle needs to be clear: that power should move upwards when, and only when, citizens are better served by its rise.

The first stop for power should be local government, which has been drastically neglected by administrations of both complexions. In the first half of the twentieth century, the London County Council raised and spent locally over three-quarters of its revenues. Centralisation, though, began in earnest in 1946 after the argument between Aneurin Bevan and Herbert Morrison over the National Insurance Act of 1946 which created the NHS. Morrison wanted municipal control of hospitals while Bevan famously declared that he wished to hear the sound of a bedpan dropping on the floor of Tredegar hospital to reverberate in the corridors of Whitehall.

The next domain for power ought to be the cities and the regions. My mother would probably not agree. She never wholly recovered from the absorption of Bury, Lancashire into Greater Manchester on 1 April 1974 under the terms of the Local Government Act 1972. She for ever after pointed out that our postcode remained BL8: Bury, Lancashire. In fact, Manchester is the best illustration in the country of what enterprising city government can do. The Manchester of my boyhood was where I learnt to appreciate the excitements of urban life but it was, with hindsight, a rather dark and forbidding place. Today, Manchester is a vibrant and prosperous city.

The transformation is in large part owed to a partnership between public authority and private capital.

We need more Manchesters because Britain is out of kilter. This is a historic problem. Back in the 1840s there was a lot of public anxiety about the north-south divide. The people of the south were worried about the hegemony of wealthy Manchester. Britain today has the same problem in reverse. We have a metropolis which is a world city and a heavy shadow cast over the provinces. It is a rare capital city anywhere in the world that is, as London is, the centre for all three sites of finance, politics and culture. If London were to declare independence, it would be the ninth-largest country in Europe.

Political governance could help to lead a rebalancing of regional economic power. There is no reason why £30 billion cannot be carved out of the budget for Whitehall and handed over to the metropolitan mayors, who should be further rewarded with additional powers. Local government in all its forms should have its capacity for raising revenue properly returned. Since the first central grant to local authorities in 1834 the proportion of money spent locally that is raised locally has dwindled. Now just 22p in every pound spent in Bury is raised in Bury. The money, though, is running out. In Bury, 35p out of every pound spent goes on social care. Next year the council will close ten of its fourteen libraries. The network of children's centres will be shut. By 2020, the council's budget will have fallen by 70 per cent since 2010. This slow strangulation has a direct impact on the esteem in which local government is held. The evidence is there in the low turnout, which was 33 per cent at the last count of the metropolitan and unitary councils in 2016. If you track turnout at local elections, which used to be very high, against this decline in local money-raising, you discover a perfect correlation. The people are rational not to vote. They have worked out that it doesn't really matter.

The next destination for legitimate power is the national state and there are many functions of modern government that are best carried out at that level. The levying of taxation and the payment of benefits are examples of the kind of uniform, universal acts that national states are good at. The central state, though, needs close attention if it is going to work. The reform of the central civil service in Whitehall is an arcane subject that moves few votes, yet if the bed pan is going to drop, some hand needs to pick it up. Whitehall's problems go so far back it is a wonder they have never been addressed. In 1906 John Maynard Keynes wrote a letter to Lytton Strachey that encapsulates everything that is wrong with the civil service. 'Yes, I am a clerk in the India Office ...', wrote Keynes, 'having passed the medical with flying colours, balls and eyesight unusually perfect they said. My marks have arrived and left me enraged. Really, knowledge seems an absolute bar to success. I have done worst in the only two subjects of which I possessed a solid knowledge – Mathematics and Economics.' More than a century later the civil service still rates Keynes's balls higher than his economics.

The term 'bureaucracy' did not at the time denote bungling or featherbedding. It meant legal rationality and efficiency, both of which were modern improvements on the arbitrary exercise of power. It was, to use Max Weber's analogy, an internal combustion engine, rather than a horse. Every review of the civil service – Northcote-Trevelyan in 1854, Fulton in 1968 – says the same thing, which is that the service is a horse run by and for the generalist amateur at the expense of the expert and the specialist. The charge sheet against the civil service is not made false because it is so sadly familiar. Mediocrity is rewarded. Risk-taking is discouraged. Civil servants are too insular. Promotion for the brilliant is too slow and demotion for the dull even slower. All the best policy analysts get promoted to become terrible managers. The skills of contracting and brokering matter much more than policy advice yet the civil service has resolutely failed to train a new cadre of recruits. Ridiculous fore-casts from the Treasury in 2007–08 were a vital factor in the complacency with which Britain sleepwalked into the banking crisis. There has, rightly, been a lot of discussion about taking responsibility for failure in banking. There has been no responsibility for failure in Whitehall, and nor is there ever.

The anachronism of ministerial responsibility, which is a nonsense in an era in which government does so much, should be abolished. Civil servants should be encouraged to come out from behind the arras that screens their decisions. The fabled independence of the civil service is a self-justifying myth. Whitehall remains the finest institution ever yet devised at seeing off change, yet change is what it needs. Each department should find its hundred brightest people and group them in cross-disciplinary teams. Half should be in charge of policy development and half in charge of monitoring and encouraging implementation. Whitehall should follow the brutal General Electric principle and show the door to the bottom 10 per cent of performers. A lot more work should be put out to tender. Senior managers should become commissioners, holding a budget and buying research and policy advice, to challenge the institutional bias on the inside. The turf war between departments can be avoided by assembling teams to treat problems on important issues, such as child obesity and troubled families, that fall down the cracks in responsibility. When a lot of policy responsibility and money raising is devolved there is no need for 5,000 civil servants in Whitehall and no need for a payroll of £16.4 billion a year. There should be fewer people at the top who are paid more. The succession for the next Permanent Secretary of the home civil service should be conducted in public, with manifestoes published and debated.

These changes would make the exercise of sovereign power more efficient at the level of the nation-state. It is, however, a fond imagining of the past to suppose that sovereign power stops here. There are many issues – climate change, immigration and organised crime are good examples – which, by their nature, require international co-operation. The extensive system of alliances in which Britain is a partner are testament to the complexity of modern state relations but also to Britain's willingness to be an active international partner. Our security is protected by membership of NATO. Britain has a series of intelligence-sharing arrangements with allies, most notably the United States. We have been signatories to the protocols of Kyoto, Copenhagen and Paris which have commanded national legislatures to take preventive and remedial action to combat climate change. We participate in the community of nations as a Security Council member of the United Nations. Since 1973, the deepest and most important of these treaty partnerships has been Britain's membership of what was then called the Common Market and is now called the EU. The debate about Britain's position with respect to the EU has been raucous and discourteous. The way to conduct it from now on is to change the point of perspective. It would be more constructive to define a desirable Europe than it would to continue the acrimony over the present one. If Britain is a member this is its reform programme. If it is not a member, these are its conditions for rejoining.

The EU is an institution that has struggled to recover from success. When war on the European mainland was part of recent memory, the meeting of former rivals in chambers of peace was a historic achievement. The creation of markets and a bonded trading bloc followed, as did decades of rule-making. At that point, having achieved so much, the EU lost its original purpose so began to search for another. With no European demos there was no appetite for a European state. A fraction of its officials have always wanted a federal organisation which would at no point have been acceptable to the electors of France and Germany, let alone the electorate in Britain. The initial energy flowed into creating a single currency in economies that were insufficiently integrated to absorb it and then into a constitutional apparatus that was rejected in successive national referendums.

The future for the EU should lie in defining those issues it is ideally placed to cover, directing its institutional features towards them. There are issues, perhaps the biggest of our time, that simply cannot be fixed without an effective EU. The movement of people across borders is the fuel for populist politics. People are more mobile than they have ever been and desperate for the more prosperous life they see, beamed into their homes or on their computer screens, in Europe. We could carry on policing this influx by means of a cruel and peremptory refusal of entry to boatloads of migrants trying to get into Italy or Greece or else we could devise a mature migration plan, managed Europe-wide. When there are no legal routes for people to travel they come illegally. The traffic in people is just one aspect of cross-border crime that defies the capacity of national law enforcement agencies. The sophisticated policing partnerships of the EU have already done a lot to close the supply lines for crime but the priority given to the issue needs to be greater. International crime comes close to a definition of the kind of problem that should be addressed at the European level. So does climate change, which respects no boundaries. A more co-ordinated environmental policy would act as a disciplinary force for those European nations whose records of compliance fall short.

The principle that the EU ought to apply, in other words, is subsidiarity – exactly the virtue it once used to advertise. European influence in legislation is both too wide and not deep enough. Its range is irritating, but in truth it leaves less of a mark, either for good or ill, than either its ardent advocates or its bilious critics suppose. The principle of subsidiarity demands a Europe that concentrates on those issues, and only those issues, that national governments ought to refer upwards. The likelihood, given that there is no turning globalisation back (and nor should there be), is that the scope of European action will grow over time. But it would grow in accordance with a clear principle that just happens to be of impeccably European origin.

Who Votes?

So, if power is to be dispersed, we need to settle who ought to wield it and how this should be done. The first priority is that everyone should be involved. The low repute of British politics can be measured in the declining turnout at elections. In 1950, 83.9 per cent of the eligible electorate voted. By 2001 it had fallen to a low of 59.4 per cent. The general election of 2017 had a turnout of just 68.7 per cent. A lack of popular interest in the issue of Europe is evinced by the fact that in the final European elections of 2014, only 35.6 per cent of the electorate thought it worthwhile to vote. It is not good for the health of politics that Theresa May can lead a Conservative government that commanded the support of just 24 per cent of the nation. In 2005 the Labour party won a 66-seat overall majority in Parliament on just 35.2 per cent of a turnout of 61.4 per cent. That gave it power to act emphatically with the active consent of no more than 21.6 per cent of the nation. It is also ridiculous and barely worthy of a serious nation, that Britain should be leaving the EU on the basis of the votes of just 37 per cent of the people. It doesn't matter which party is the beneficiary at the general election and it doesn't matter which side won the referendum; these numbers are too low and the legitimacy they afford is too weak.

I am haunted by the image of the cars carrying the ballot boxes in procession to the count. The beauty of the idea is clearly not universally felt, yet the transaction behind it really matters. And it is the thinnest of threads between a citizen and the common wealth to ask people to vote. It is therefore time to do just that; it is time to make voting compulsory. People are, of course, free not to be interested. It is reasonable to say that voting is a civic right but not a civic duty. However, all laws trade a small fraction of individual liberty for the public good. Tax is not voluntary. Since 1870 it has been mandatory to send children to school. We have at times conscripted men to fight in the army. The state commands us to attend court to do jury service. Plenty of nations ask this much of their citizens without thereby cancelling liberty. Voting is compulsory in Argentina, Belgium, Brazil, Cyprus, Ecuador, Liechtenstein, Luxembourg, Peru, Singapore and Uruguay, though the most comparable example is Australia. Since 1924, enrolling and voting in federal elections and referendums in Australia has been mandatory, punishable, without a valid reason, with a $20 fine, though it is still open to the Australian voter to spoil the ballot paper. There is no doubt that compulsion raises turnout. The 2013 federal election had a turnout of 93.3 per cent. If the 2016 European referendum had granted such a mandate the argument over its outcome might be less vicious than it is.

As a general rule, compulsion ought to be avoided. The more that a nation lives by tacit agreement and dialogue the better it will flourish. Yet the interference with freedom to ensure that people cast a vote is trivial; the benefit great. Compulsory voting has three virtues: it would allow government to focus on chronic problems; it would change policy priorities for the better; and it would ensure that the concerns of every citizen carry equal weight.

It is a common flaw of democracies that their time spans are too short. The returns on social mobility policies come in too late. Infrastructure spending pays no early dividend. Climate change can await a receding tomorrow. The imbalance between the generations is one of the chronic problems of our time yet the coalition government exempted pensioners from its austerity programme. The unsurprising reason was that older people vote in greater numbers than younger people. In the 2015 general election the Conservatives beat Labour by 47 per cent to 23 per cent among the over sixty-fives. Labour did have a clear lead among people under the age of thirty-four but only 43 per cent of that cohort voted; turnout among the over sixty-fives was 78 per cent. A government that faced a compulsory vote would be forced to take a wider view of the public interest rather than merely buying off its most loyal section.

Political priorities change in an instant when the whole electorate votes. With the threatened pressure from a younger battalion, it will be impossible for politicians to ignore the nation's poor market for rental housing. Climate change will become a more salient political issue. A low turnout, in a first-past-the-post electoral system, has a baleful effect on political campaigning. It makes obvious sense to concentrate on people who are likely to vote, in places that are likely to alter the result. If you are a young person in a safe seat, don't expect to see any political campaigners because you don't really count. This is why the Conservatives and Labour are all over Bury like a cheap suit at election time. They spend a lot less of their time in most of Manchester, where Labour victories are taken for granted.

The bill to introduce compulsory voting should include a clause to fold sixteen- and seventeen-year-olds into the electorate. There are some commonly heard bad arguments for this reform and we need to ignore them. It is not relevant to voting that at the age of sixteen a young person can, with the permission of their parents, get married or join the Army. It is permissible to buy chocolate liqueurs at sixteen but you have to wait until eighteen to buy fireworks. A sixteen-year-old can own a pet but cannot legally get a tattoo. Is any of this instructive for the democratic franchise? If we prize consistency over relevance then the common age of consent might as well be eighteen as sixteen. That would at least keep minors out of prison and off the military frontline.

In the end this is a judgement about whether, in general and on average, sixteen-year-olds are mature enough to cast a ballot. I can furnish a sorry example of the case against. The general election of 1983 took place twenty-four days after my sixteenth birthday. As someone who has in his time helped to send Jeremy Corbyn and Diane Abbott to the Houses of Parliament, I am more capable than most of an electoral error. The restriction of the franchise to eighteen-year-olds, however, did save me from the indignity of having voted for Michael Foot, estimable in so much apart from political leadership, to be the nation's Prime Minister. Yet we do not give people the vote because we define what is right. In conjunction with a serious civics curriculum in schools, the mandatory franchise should now be extended.

How Should They Vote?

It would take more than extending the franchise, of course, to make the British electoral system fair. In the two general elections of 1970 and the further two in 1974, my parents voted Conservative in Rotherham, South Yorkshire. For what good it did them. The voters of Rotherham returned Brian O'Malley to Parliament for Labour at every one of those elections, with more than 60 per cent of the vote each time. In the October 1974 election my parents were among a mere 8,840 hopeful souls who cast a forlorn, wasted vote for Richard Hambro, the humiliated Conservative candidate. Just before they left to take us back to my mum's home town of Bury, they would have voted, in June 1976, in the Rotherham by-election caused by the death from complications in brain surgery of Brian O'Malley. Douglas Hinckley did rather better for the Tories than Richard Hambro had, taking 35 per cent of the vote. He still lost comfortably to Stan Crowther, who retained the seat for Labour with just over 50 per cent of the vote.

It cannot have been easy being a Conservative in the socialist republic of South Yorkshire. For all I know, my parents may have worked out that the effective value of their vote was precisely zero and failed to show up. I doubt it, as they both regarded voting as a civic duty. Yet they never once affected the outcome. Indeed, in a lifetime of dutiful voting my mother only backed a winner three times, in 1983, 1987 and 1992, when she voted for the Conservative Alastair Burt in Bury. Considering that she voted in fourteen general elections, she wasn't very good at it. My dad was even worse. He only ever voted for a winner once, in 1983. After that he made the catastrophic error of moving to Heywood, which weighed the Labour vote rather than counted it. Why do we treat civic-minded people as if their vote didn't matter?

The British refusal to create a decent electoral system is peerlessly exemplified by the Duke of Wellington. His nickname, 'the Iron Duke', derives from the fact that he had to put girding on the windows of his London residence Apsley House to stop protesters smashing them after he tried to the prevent the passage of the 1832 Reform Act. The case for the British electoral system is essentially the same as the case against. A complex result gets translated into a seat allocation that exaggerates both the victory of the winner and the defeat of the loser. This provides, according to your viewpoint, either strong executive government or manifest unfairness. In fact, it provides both – strength at the expense of fairness. Better to be unfair and stable than fair and unstable, runs the argument, and there is, indeed, a case for that. Unpopular governments that have been in power too long get unceremoniously kicked out. Small parties are not given too much weight.

The deficiency in fairness can be justified if, but only if, the system does in fact produce emphatic victories. However, first-past-the-post is much less effective than that. We pretend that coalition governments are foreign events that the smarter British system cunningly avoids. The evidence of the twentieth century hardly upholds that view. At times of peril, when efficient government matters most and its influence is the greatest, Britain has sought the comfort of more than a single tribe. During the First World War and in its immediate wake, from 1915 to 1922, Herbert Asquith and David Lloyd George led coalitions. When the horror of war returned, it was a coalition between the Conservative and Labour parties that organised the war effort between 1940 and 1945.

Aside from military conflict the worst catastrophe a nation can face is economic collapse and it is telling that the political response to the two steepest falls in the twentieth and twenty-first centuries – the financial crashes of 1929 and 2008 – was in both instances coalition government. Between 1931 and 1940 a National Government was formed, led by the Conservatives but including three Labour members. In 2010, David Cameron and Nick Clegg began a coalition that lasted the full five-year term. Disraeli once said that Britain does not love coalitions. When there is a mess to be cleared or a danger to be averted that does not seem to be true. Taken together, these instances account for a full quarter of a century.

The nature of governments is anyway never fully determined by electoral systems. Australia uses the Alternative Vote but has had just a single hung Parliament in thirty-eight elections over seventy years. Spain has a proportional system in which coalitions are rare but coalitions occur regularly in Canada, which uses first-past-the-post. Britain is already, in any case, probably the most varied electoral nation on earth. We use the Additional Member system for the Scottish Parliament, the Welsh Assembly and the London Assembly. The Northern Irish Assembly, meanwhile, is elected by the Single Transferable Vote. Besides, the British system has not produced a truly decisive outcome since 2005. When the politics of the nation are locked, when there is no good option, a system that relies on exaggerating small differences is truly inappropriate. A far more mature response to this is not to lament coalition government but to learn to weigh its virtues.

As someone who once spent three days negotiating with an adviser to Gordon Brown about the inclusion of the word 'and' in a policy document, I have always thought that the real hatred takes places within political tribes rather than between them. Though the Conservative and Liberal Democrat coalition had its moments of tension between 2010 and 2015, it was not, in its own terms, an unsuccessful government. Leave aside whether what it did was desirable or not; it was able to carry out its programme. Indeed the severe, and largely justified, criticism of austerity is predicated on the fact that the government was strong enough to carry it out.

This is not the habitual criticism. Coalitions are alleged to be congenitally weak, morbid and prone to collapse. They are said to be fatally weakened by the tension between their two impulses – the one a need for unity between parties of different stamps, the other the desire of each to preserve a distinctive identity. The experience of 2010 to 2015 suggests the opposite may be closer to the point. The need to ensure formal agreement between coalition partners revived some of the Cabinet committees and arcane procedures of the British state. There was limited but licensed disagreement between the two parties and the inevitable disputes, which happen in all single-party government, were conducted in a better spirit. Politics is the negotiation of plural difference. Coalition government is a mature recognition of that fact. Tribal identity is a refusal to acknowledge it.

The charge that should be levelled against the 2010 coalition is that it promised so much more than it delivered. The spirit in which agreement was initially reached, culminating in David Cameron and Nick Clegg's famous press conference in the Downing Street rose garden, seemed, in the fleeting sunshine of May 2010, to herald a new kind of politics. There was a sense, vague and inchoate though it was, that something new and exciting in the conduct of politics was struggling to be born. Yet the moment passed and the opportunity was lost. 'Footfalls echo in the memory', wrote T. S. Eliot in *Burnt Norton*, 'Down the passage which we did not take/Towards the door we never opened/Into the rose-garden.'

There is another door that never gets opened; the door across the Central Lobby that runs between the House of Commons and the House of Lords. Though the lower house of the British Parliament is not elected in a fair way the upper house is not elected at all. This has to change. It is a bedrock principle of a democracy that institutions with the authority to draft legislation must be representative. All complaints about how well the House of Lords works and how expert its members might be are beside the point. A parliamentary chamber in a democracy should be an elected body. 'We must choose between anomaly and democracy', wrote Walter Bagehot in 1864. To which the answer must be obvious. The House of Lords is indefensible.

The simplest answer has been supplied, remarkably enough, by Billy Bragg. The Lords should be elected on the same day, in the same election, as the Commons. Everyone's vote should count twice. The first count takes place under a version of the Alternative Vote, to bring more fairness to the House of Commons. The second count allocates seats in the reformed Senate in strict arith-metical proportion to the votes in the country. If the Senate had 300 representatives, the Conservatives would currently have 127 (42.4 per cent), Labour would have 120 (40 per cent) and the Liberal Democrats would have 22 (7.4 per cent). The Scottish National Party would have 9 members of the upper chamber of a country they do not believe in and UKIP would have 5. Any party which won more than 0.3 per cent would be entitled to a Senate seat. Some of them might conceivably be unpleasant but it is the task of politics to defeat them in argument, not just rig the system against them.

This new second chamber would have the necessary trait of not being a replica of the first. The Salisbury Convention, by which the House of Lords yields to measures that were contained in general election manifestoes, would apply unchanged. The new House would have a mandate from the electorate but, because it is indirect, it would not usurp the supremacy of the Commons. The constitutional balance would have been preserved and democracy would have been introduced in a way that makes every vote count. And it would all be very simple to do. Billy Bragg once promised that he didn't want to change the world. He wasn't looking for a new England. He might have found one anyway.

The Caucus Race

This hybrid scheme is a way of making anomaly and democracy join hands. There is one anomaly that it would be a shame to lose though and that is the cadre of peers who sit under no party insignia. Under the new system, members would be selected from lists provided by the political parties. Though it is perfectly conceivable that a fraction, let us say a fifth, of the seats could be reserved for independent members, there is always the risk that the upper house is turned into what Michael Foot memorably called 'a seraglio of eunuchs'.

Foot's vivid phrase is a biting condemnation, richly deserved, of the main political parties. Parties are indispensable institutions in a representative democracy, yet we need to guard against their becoming too powerful. There is a particular danger that their activists, the people who simply turn up, will wield more power than they warrant. In 'Caucus-Race and a Long Tale', the third chapter of *Alice's Adventures in Wonderland*, Lewis Carroll presents a scene that will be familiar to anyone who attends the meetings of a political party. Alice gathers all the animals on the riverbank to discuss how to get dry. The Mouse gives an irrelevant, boring lecture on William the Conqueror and a Dodo says the answer is to hold a caucus-race in which everyone runs around pointlessly in a circle. My mind goes back to meetings of Islington North constituency Labour party in 1990. The local MP, a nice young man of no great ambition called Jeremy, resolved to send another stiff letter to the United Nations, on constituency headed notepaper, about East Timor. I was deputed to compose the angry missive, which I did, in a state of high dudgeon. Weeks passed without a reply. By the time of the next monthly meeting of Islington North constituency Labour party the Secretary-General of the United Nations had, inexplicably, still not replied, let alone acted. Undeterred, we resolved to write again, this time an even stiffer letter. The capacity of letters from Islington North constituency Labour party to change the course of world events was not an issue we paused to consider. We await their reply.

The obscure obsessions of political parties would be merely farcical if they did not matter. One day before

2022 it is probable that 125,000 members of the Conservative party will choose Britain's next Prime Minister. This is a privilege that ought to be removed. Changing a Prime Minister within a Parliament should trigger a general election. The fiction that we elect a party not a Prime Minister stands no scrutiny in this presidential age. For the moment, though, party activists are the most powerful tiny tribe in politics. The total membership of British political parties amounts to just 1 per cent of the electorate. Thirty years ago it was four times that, which was already not very many. This grants a privileged position to those who run around in the circle of the caucus-race. It is obvious that the old model of the political party is defunct. The only way to change this is to join up; an influx of moderates makes a party moderate. So let the cry ring out to the army of the uninterested and the cavalry of those with better things to do. Hurry to the caucus-race; you have nothing to lose but your evenings.

An incidental but not trivial benefit of more public involvement in politics would be that the political parties raise more of their own money. They are not, however, ever likely to be wholly self-funding. Money and politics make a toxic brew and the lasting damage caused by instances such as that of David Chaytor is that they encourage the idea that British politics is essentially corrupt. The Electoral Reform Society (ERS) found that 75 per cent of British people believe big donors have too much influence on our political parties. But of all the democracies in the world, Britain has some of the fewest problems with financial corruption. The reason David Lloyd George's sale of honours in 1922 is infamous is that such instances are so rare. Yet party funding *is* a mess, wealthy donors *do* have too great an influence and there *is* an obvious connection between gifts and places in the House of Lords. We can deal with the second side of that equation by electing the upper chamber but we still have to deal with the first.

There is one obviously clean way of paying for politics and nobody likes it. It is standard practice in most countries for taxpayers to fund politics directly, on the grounds that political parties perform an important constitutional function. In Germany it is written into the federal constitution that any party gaining more than 1 per cent of the vote is entitled to state funding up to a maximum of 50 per cent of its income. About a third of party income in Germany comes from taxpayers and it costs them €1.66 each, about the price of a cup of coffee. Popular outrage after a series of funding scandals led the French, in 1988, to introduce public funding. The Australians did the same in 1984 and the Canadians in 2003. The sky does not appear to have caved in anywhere.

Indeed, we do have a meagre version of state funding ourselves. The public grant to the official Opposition, known as Short money in the House of Commons and Cranborne money in the House of Lords, was the source, for the Conservative party, of more money than it received in all its private donations between 2001 and 2003. The state kept the Conservative party afloat, and quite right too. It then did the same for Labour in its dog days of opposition. The argument about the public funding of political parties is not whether we should introduce it. It's about whether we should extend it. The case for public funding of political parties is justified because it is a bad idea whose every alternative is worse. It is even less appealing than state funding that 90 per cent of the Labour party's funding comes from the trades unions and that this hands far too much power to some of the movement's less public-spirited leaders. Public money also has to be a less venal source of political support than the hedge-funders and assorted manufacturing plutocrats who foot the bills for the Conservative party. The consequence of relying on private wealth is that we will risk periodic scandals in our politics, with the resultant fall in esteem of the whole estate. In politics money always smells, but politics costs money like everything else and we have two options: pay up or shut up.

Security and Freedom

Constitutional theory is as dry as a stone wall. It will need distinctive signature policies to symbolise the fact that it really matters. The best way to dramatise the importance of dispersing power is to scatter its citadels. The crumbling parliamentary estate is about to undergo a major refit and MPs will decamp to the Department of Health during the renovation. A much more imaginative solution would be for Parliament to move to Birmingham. Then, when the Palace of Westminster is ready, MPs should return south and the new upper chamber should stay north. The only physical connection between the two chambers of Parliament is that a clerk in a wig carries a manuscript of any disputed bill between them. He could send an email. Or, if he is desperate to do it in person, get the train. That can be an incentive to get on with the high-speed rail link. Large sections of the civil service could be relocated to Bristol, Sheffield, Leeds and Newcastle. The monarchy could take a lead by moving most of its operations north where it could reside in a modern palace purpose-built by Daniel Libeskind on a site by the old Manchester ship canal.

These renovated institutions would be part of a polity that should, in the end, command our support. There are occasions when the contest between politics and its alternative is tragically dramatised. On 22 March 2017, Khalid Masood drove his car into passers-by on Westminster Bridge before attacking a policeman guarding the entrance to the Houses of Parliament. Four people were murdered. An attack like that pits the open society against its enemies. It is a reminder that preserving the security of its citizens is the first duty of the state. The battle of the state against terror is a perennial battle that began in earnest in Britain when Sir William Harcourt established the precursor to Special Branch, to deal with Irish republicans, in the 1880s.

On 7 July 2005 I was in the Cabinet meeting, as an observer, when an official interrupted to bring in an important notice to Charles Clarke, Home Secretary. Cabinet proceedings paused because it was apparent that something was wrong. The Home Secretary read the note silently and then said, calmly but very gravely, that three bombs had exploded (there was later a fourth) on London transport. In the ensuing hours it was grimly impressive to witness the state apparatus at work. Coroners, the police, local authorities, pathologists and the London resilience team were all engaged. The response to terror attacks is now, alas, well-practised. However, unless we all consent to live in a security cage there are no intelligence operations, no local resilience forums or Cabinet Office guidelines that can guarantee that a fantasist drunk on ideology will not drive a car into pedestrians in the name of whatever eschatological fantasy he thinks affords him an alibi for murder.

No part of the state apparatus matters more to citizens than Robert Peel's legacy, the police force, the authority of law and order. The police is one of those forces which, unless acted upon, remains exactly unchanged. By the end of the twentieth century crime was 60 times higher than at the start. Even allowing for population growth, it was 30 times higher. The nature of crime changed as much as the volume. The prospect of being burgled receded but knife and gun crime flourished on urban streets. People-trafficking took place across national boundaries, money laundering snuck into invisible bank ledgers and identity theft took place in cyberspace. Faced with this abundance of new problems, the effectiveness of policing has declined. Over the past 50 years the crime detection rate has fallen from 47 per cent to 28 per cent. Britain has a high crime rate at least in part because the odds of getting away with it are so good.

Modern policing needs fewer uniformed officers and more detectives. Bright graduates should be recruited into 'Police First', a replica of the 'Teach First' scheme which has done so much for teaching. The force needs to open up to senior personnel from other professions and it needs to become much more specialised. Identity theft and fraud, for example, should be broken off and given to specialist agencies. That would allow local forces to concentrate on the recidivists on their patch. More than half of all crime is committed by 100,000 persistent offenders and the police know very well who they are.

These changes should be accompanied by prison reform. Prison both works and does not work. It works to punish malfeasants, to protect the public by keeping dangerous characters off the street and to reduce crime by locking up habitual perpetrators. But prison also does not work because half of all inmates offend again within a year of being released. That is hardly surprising given that they receive no rehabilitation. Nobody is writing *Pilgrim's Progress* inside. Too many of them can't read it, let alone write it. Yet prison has become the default setting of criminal justice policy. A quarter of a century ago there were 44,000 people incarcerated; now there are

85,000. And we need to stop jailing the wrong people. There are three distinct types of prisoner: immature boys, people in dire need of help and career criminals. Young men comprise half the prison population and half of those stays could be avoided if community orders were more effective. A further 30 per cent of prisoners should be discharged at once because they are people for whom prison is the wrong place. Nobody with a mental health problem or in the grip of drug or alcohol addiction should be behind bars. And it no more makes sense to imprison 1,300 people for defaulting on fines than it did when Charles Dickens wrote *Little Dorrit*. That leaves a fifth of the prison population who are hardened career criminals and that is where the police effort should be concentrated.

Effective law and order is the bedrock of a liberal polity. If your favourite books are Erskine May on parliamentary procedure and John Stuart Mill's *On Liberty*, no twisting can turn those liberal tomes into a deranged pretext for murdering a police officer guarding a democratic chamber. It is a stark reminder of why we need a defence of politics and why our politics needs to be worthy of that defence. Democracy, said Albert Camus, is the system that relies on the wisdom of people who know that they do not know everything. We endure periodic reminders, paid in the currency of terror, of what happens when people who will not admit compromise seek to assert their will and impose their certainty on others. A good liberal democracy is a historic achievement but it would be complacent to say that it is working well. Politics has to make people feel powerful and effective and right now it does neither. Under the common wealth it will do both.

4

POWER
FAILURE

An English Sentence

My mother always liked to tell people the story of how she taught me to read by making me slowly decipher *The Times*. Writing this book, as I did, in the *Times* room of a library, surrounded by paper copies of the newspaper going back to 1785, I looked up what I might have been reading on my third birthday when my mother started to open the door for me into the wonders of English script.

The Times of 16 May 1970 describes a past that is still present. The two editorials were about the Irish border and the European negotiation, exactly the issues of the hour as I was writing this chapter. 'South of the Border' described the descent of Irish politics into a border skirmish. 'The Negotiating Timetable' was a reflection on the poor state of Britain's attempts to talk itself into Europe: 'the Common Market debate could become much hotter after an election than in the run-up to one', wrote the leader writer on behalf of the Editor, as if in preparation for being a *Times* columnist almost half a century later. On the opinion page, Auberon Waugh lamented the 'plasticine politics' in which dubious personality cults prevailed over a serious account of government policy. It could all have been written yesterday.

Even if, at the age of three, I did not really read the newspaper, still less understand it, my mother certainly did. She would have bridled at the report of Harold Wilson's plans for a £70 million boost to pensions. She bridled at anything Harold Wilson did. All her life she excoriated him for breaking a promise to the teachers, the instance of which I have never been able to establish. My mother would also have reacted badly to the report that the benefits bill was set to rise. She would have reacted, I imagine, exactly as her father would have done, with disdain. My grandfather often told the story of his own father refusing state benefits because they were hand-outs. Thomas Taylor felt that welfare was a badge of shame. His task was to provide for his own family.

My mother would have approved more of the plan for the education of factory workers, though, as a primary school teacher who refused to strike, she would not have been sympathetic to the report of a pay protest in the civil service. As a mother already quietly ambitious for the education of her son I am sure too that she would have sniffed at the snobbery of the literary critic F. R. Leavis, who made the headlines in *The Times* on my third birthday with his typical view, still heard in the debate today, that widening access to universities would inevitably dilute the quality of the teaching.

The Times, as a place where the national conversation is conducted, was full, in 1970 as it is now, of serious public questions such as these. Beneath these headlines lie deep questions about how we organise our common lives as citizens. The public services, funded through a common treasury, are the places in which our equal citizenship is recognised and enacted. They organise vital functions of life which are either best provided at scale or which are owed to the citizen as a matter of right, irrespective of their capacity to pay. We do not think of buying care or education in the same terms as buying baked beans. When we suffer we are all equal. That insight is, in turn, protected by the fact that, in healthcare, the cash nexus is invisible and money obeys the clinical need, not the income of the unwell. It is through the funding mechanism, in which a tiny fraction of my income is transferred to pay for the care of someone less fortunate, that the beautiful equity of the NHS is preserved.

My reading material as a three-year-old was a primer in this ethos of public service. The discussions my parents had at home, as Conservative-voting teachers from working-class families, were an instruction in the virtue of professional service. My mother taught generations of young children – first the white working class in Rotherham in South Yorkshire and then boys and girls of Pakistani and Bangladeshi heritage in Bury – to articulate an English sentence, the gift she gave me too. It was a vocation, governed by an idea of service, a noble and generous idea without which a liberal democracy cannot function. The common wealth will need to define and update the idea of the public service ethos which has lately seemed tattered and torn but without which all instances are reduced to transactions. This is the subject of the public conversation relayed in *The Times* that helped me learn to read and relayed in *The Times* that helped me learn to write.

The public service ethos of the common wealth should embody four important principles. First, the earlier we act collectively the better because prevention is preferable to cure, as well as being a lot less expensive. Second, the process of educating individuals is critical in order to ensure adults have the capability of taking control. Third, power and control should be vested as close to the individual as possible and should always be organised with the best interest of the citizen in mind. Fourth and last, prior contribution should be recognised; citizens who have added to the stock of the nation should be rewarded for having done so. A public service ethos that respects prevention, capability, control and contribution is the way to grant power to people and produce results that those same people define as being good.

Give Me the Child of Three

The child who is taught to read at the age of three from the opinion pages in *The Times* is being taught at the moment of maximum receptivity. He is being granted the gift of reading that opens a door into the palace of knowledge. Inadvertently but definitively at the same time his likelihood of going to prison is being drastically reduced and his opportunities in employment far enhanced. A whole drama of unhappy events will never afflict him because of the initial care and attention lavished on him.

There is a vast body of evidence to attest to the fact that the major problems of British social policy can be prevented before they have the chance to do their harm. Yet public services in Britain are organised as emergency services, frantically remedying defects that neglect has allowed to flourish. The NHS, for example, has developed as an illness-treatment service and it is so over-burdened that it does not do a great deal of prevention. Yet the examples of immunisation, reduced smoking rates and compulsory seat belts in cars show what a difference it can make. Think of all the diseases not contracted, the morbidity avoided, the injuries never suffered because of these policies of prevention. Imagine the welfare state and public services reconstructed around the principle of prevention. Think of how much unnecessary suffering would be avoided and then, to be more mercenary about it, think too of the vast cost that would be avoided.

The potential of prevention is enormous. For example, only 1 per cent of children live in a care home yet they account for 40 per cent of those who end up in secure training centres and young offender institutions. Half the children in care will spend some time in prison and, at any one moment, children who once lived in a care home make up a quarter of the prison population. Every prison place costs £35,000 a year and the budget for care homes is nearly £1 billion. It does not have to be like this. In many other European countries the state is not shy to intervene earlier than we do in Britain. Very young children are taken into care where the support offered by a trained workforce is extensive and of the highest calibre. We know that the children who go into care in Britain are below the average level of education for their age group and we know that the outcome of this will be bad, yet we do nothing to correct it. In Denmark, Germany and Norway they act and the results are impressive. Children who go through the care system in these nations are more likely to stay on at school and get better qualifications. In Denmark, the approach is to make a children's home more like a family home. Workers engage much more emotionally with children and perform tasks together. Children are involved in decisions about their lives and encouraged to sort out tensions and disputes. They live in a home, not a warehouse.

Good early care also helps to prevent the descent into drug abuse. There could be as many as 35,000 prisoners whose felony is in some way drug-related. In addition, about half of burglary, robbery and vehicle theft are drug-related. So is a lot of violent crime. The pain and anguish caused to, but mostly by, drug addicts is vast and it can be prevented. Twenty years ago, the National Institute on Drug Abuse in the USA identified sixteen ways that we know how to help those on the road to addiction. We know too that children of addicted parents are twice as likely to become addicts themselves. Neither of these insights has been acted on. The template is Switzerland where, from the 1970s on, there was an explosion in the use of heroin. Toughening the law made it worse, so the Swiss changed course. Heroin Assisted Therapy (HAT) creates a legal and strictly regulated market in clean heroin, clean needles, medical supervision and therapy. The scheme has led to substantial improvements in the well-being of participants and major reductions in their drug use. The criminal activity of participants declined markedly and they were far more likely to remain in stable housing and a steady job. The criminal production supply line of heroin is interrupted with all the benefits, civil and financial, that implies.

The problems of children in care and drug users can both be cured later in life, though at much greater expense and with far greater difficulty. There are some conditions, such as dementia, for which there is no cure, which makes prevention all the more vital. We have learnt that if we can reduce diabetes mellitus, midlife hypertension and depression then we can delay the onset of dementia and, in some cases, prevent it entirely. In the UK today there are 750,000 people with dementia. By 2040 there will be 1.32 million. The costs to the individual are measured in the dreadfully diminished quality of life and the costs to the taxpayer run to £10.5 billion a year. The bill will be £18 billion a year by 2040. If we did all that can be done to mitigate the risks of dementia the total savings between now and then could be as much as £40 billion.

There is in all of this an intractable funding problem. You have to keep paying for the cure while you shift the money to prevention. In due course there will be a saving, but in politics it can be difficult to wait for due course to arrive. As a result we all collude in a sub-optimal outcome in which we remedy a problem rather than treat its roots. Here, unless we are prepared to borrow vast amounts, Robert Lowe could come to the rescue again. After his revolutionary impact on company law, Lowe pioneered the idea of 'payment by results'. The future for funding prevention may reside in a blend of Lowe's two great ideas. The fledgling idea of social finance, cleverly deployed, can help to solve social problems. Social Impact Bonds (SIBs) have been used to reduce reoffending among male prisoners, to keep rough sleepers off the streets and to get young people back into work. The idea is that investors put money into public policy schemes in which their return is linked to the fixing of a social problem. If the objectives can be isolated and clarified, it may be possible to raise on the private markets the seed funding that the state will struggle to commit. This is a source of new money which allows experiments in policy with no risk to public funds and it could be the way to finance more free schools, to improve the conditions of children in care, to tackle substance addiction, to reduce the visits that old people make to hospital and to manage chronic conditions such as asthma and diabetes. We simply do not take prevention seriously. In the common wealth, we will.

The essence of all prevention, of course, is that it makes sense to act earlier rather than later. The earlier, indeed, the better. Children can be prevented from going into care and can enjoy a better education at home if their parents are only helped to do the toughest and most vital job of their lives, which is to be parents. There is no need for kids to turn up on their first day of school totally unequipped to learn. Children from families with criminal parents are significantly more likely to become criminals themselves. There is a chain of causation in difficult lives which we have to break. The most reliable way of predicting social position at the age of nineteen, for example, is to look at attainment at the age of sixteen. The best way to predict attainment at sixteen is simply to check attainment at eleven. The pupils who do best at eleven are, with notable exceptions to whom we give too much publicity, the same as the pupils who do best at seven. This recalls the famous Jesuit maxim of Ignatius Loyola: 'give me the child of seven and I will show you the man'. In fact, Loyola was optimistic. The most reliable way, in Britain, to predict the good performers at the age of seven is to seek out their test results at the age of three and a half.

The economist James Heckman has demonstrated that you make more difference to the life of a child in its earliest years than at any other time. Yet the pattern of public spending in Britain conspires to defy this elementary principle. Public spending designed to provide equal life chances would be heavy at the start of life and extensive during schooling. Giving priority to the young is exactly the pattern of resources practised within any loving family. Yet in the collective welfare state, public spending takes off just at the moment it ceases to make much difference. There is, at current prices, £750 billion available every year and it is allocated with no account taken of the efficacy of each pound spent. Look, for example, at the journey that the new-born takes through the welfare state. After the maternity ward come the visits of the health visitor and the early attention of the GP. We know, from a vast corpus of work, that this is the moment of brain formation. We know that though life chances may not be set in stone they are certainly set in motion. It is precisely when it matters most that the welfare state backs off.

By the age of seven I had been through four years of reading Auberon Waugh in *The Times*. Every few months my mother would take out her book of comprehension tests and check that my reading age was far enough in excess of my actual age. There are too many parents, however, who are not equipped to be their children's first and best teacher. The state should act *in loco parentis* in such cases. There is nothing wrong with the nanny state when it is actually acting as a nanny. In fact, it needs to be more than that; it needs to be a teacher. Parenting classes are a proven way to help people become better parents and they should be vastly expanded. Child care needs to be more than baby-minding. Child care policy serves two aims but they call for different approaches. If the chief aim is to permit mothers to go back to work, then safely guarding their children will suffice. If, however, the aim is to enhance the status of the child, as it ought to be, then it calls for qualified staff. They are worth the expense. The best estimate is that every pound spent at this point in a child's life saves the unnecessary expenditure of seven pounds later.

When the priority for expenditure is in the earlier years of life, we might start to get university education into perspective. Tuition fees have become the graveyard of political careers but public funding of undergraduates is a sadly regressive policy. The bulk of the advantage of a degree passes to the graduate, whose lifetime earnings will on average be £400,000 more than a non-graduate's. Rather than spend £2 billion of taxpayers' money each year, the best way to fund university education is through a capped graduate tax. This scheme would require no fees to be charged up front and the cost would be recouped, like any other tax, from the payroll. Payments would begin only when the student starts to earn more than £21,000 and the rate of interest – again as with any other tax – would be progressively tapered. There is only one way in which this scheme would not be like tax, namely that, once the liability has been removed, the graduate would stop paying it. Or, if the full amount had not been met after thirty years, the debt would be written off.

This plan ensures a dedicated income stream, and therefore academic autonomy, for the universities. The chief virtue of the plan, though, is that it already exists. The existing tuition fees regime is, in effect, a capped graduate tax. It places the main financial burden on the beneficiaries, although only if they can afford to pay it back. Universities do need to meet tougher standards on access to justify their fees and maintenance grants need to be reinstated but the distraction of tuition fees should not dominate our thinking. We need to concentrate on those children who are not being taught to read out of the pages of *The Times*.

Capable Citizens

There are, alas, too many of those who are left to their own devices. The blood feuds of British education mean that children are being failed by a system that is inadequately tailored to their needs. The British schools system is the best in the world for the top stratum of society. It is much less effective at providing anything adequate for those children who are not candidates for Russell Group universities. Britain has one of the largest gaps between the higher and the lower achievers in the developed world. More than 13,000 children leave school at sixteen every year with nothing to their name and as many again don't even attend the exams. A further 10,000 every year gain a single pass in an academic subject, which counts the same as nothing to an employer. A quarter of all children don't manage a single A or B grade at GCSE and the overwhelming majority of them come from working-class families.

We become capable people through a process of education. By no means all of that education takes place formally in the classroom, but much of it does. One of the philosophical foundations of the common wealth is that citizens should be granted more control over their own lives. For that control to be real, people need to be given the capabilities to wield it. A better educated democracy is a better democracy as well as a happier and a more prosperous society. Yet education policy in Britain has been a catalogue of failures going all the way back to 1944. It was in that year that R. A. Butler's Education Act introduced a tripartite system of grammar schools, technical schools and secondary moderns. The split had classical origins in Plato's *Republic* in which the Guardians, the purveyors of wisdom, control the State. They are aided, in strict hierarchical order, by the Auxiliaries, who keep the peace, primarily over the Producers who, distinguished by their bodily appetites, do the drudgery that keeps society moving.

There were two serious mistakes in Butler's system. The first was the split between grammars and secondary moderns. The selection of a tiny grammar school elite, at the premature age of eleven, and the dumping of the rest into secondary moderns, stamped 'second-rate' on the heads of too many capable children. The case for grammar schools, which despite all the evidence to the contrary, is regularly repeated, is an illusion. The grammar schools served social mobility but they did not cause it. At the height of their popularity, only 1 per cent of the grammar school pupils who gained two A-levels came from the skilled working class. Michael Young caught the politics perfectly in *The Rise of the Meritocracy*: 'Every selection of one is a rejection of many.' Comprehensive schools were thus the product, not of the ideological fantasies of Tony Crosland, but of the demands of middle-class parents who hated secondary moderns.

Then came Butler's second mistake. Very few of the promised technical schools were ever built. The task of a functioning education system is to recognise the variation of talent and nurture its many splendid forms. Too many pupils in Britain are neglected for want of the appropriate curriculum. By the age of fourteen, we know what children can do, and so do they. At the age of fourteen we should be giving children the opportunity to get off the academic road if that's what they want to do. There should be a major expansion of technical education, long promised but never delivered. The university technical schools (UTCs) created by the former Conservative Education Secretary Lord Baker of Dorking are a template for what is needed. Students start at fourteen and study for diplomas aimed at the workplace, such as engineering, alongside the basics of English, mathematics and science.

The pupils following the academic route have been led a merry dance too. Before 1951 students took a course towards a school certificate followed, for the gifted who made it through a further two years, by the higher school certificate. In 1951, the two school certificates were replaced by the O-level for sixteen-year-olds and the A-level for eighteen-year-olds. Then, in 1965, to cater for the less academically able pupils who were struggling with the pass-or-fail nature of the O-level, Harold Wilson's government introduced the certificate of secondary education (CSE). This rapidly became an O-level of lesser virtue. The O-level catered for the top 20 per cent; the CSE for the next 40 per cent. Within this system, the rest, a further 40 per cent, went nowhere. In 1988, the Thatcher government tried to integrate all students into a single examination at sixteen, the general certificate of secondary education (GCSE).

When the leaving age was sixteen or below it made sense to ensure that pupils did not leave school without a certificate. These days, the slim justification for public examinations at sixteen has disappeared and it is time to abolish them. Most countries do not bother and neither should we. There is no need for the curriculum to come to a full stop at the age of sixteen and then start over again. Those who are taking the academic path should be given two options that culminate at eighteen. The A-level is appropriate for those who are ready to specialise early.

A *baccalaureat* curriculum with a wider range should be offered to those who, at the age of sixteen, are not ready to rule out either the humanities or the sciences in preference to the other. For all students maths and English would be compulsory through to sixteen, as would a detailed and sophisticated course of civics which would be a primer in the democratic institutions and procedures of the common wealth.

Take Back Control

A revised curriculum hands power to the neglected group for whom the status quo offers nothing. In the common wealth as much control as possible should be in the hands of the citizens. In education this means giving parents meaningful choices about the school their child attends, and it also means ensuring that teachers can run schools well for the benefit of their pupils. The best way to expand choice is to increase the range of types of school. A viable technical curriculum will bring a cohort into the fold of education who are currently poorly served. But there needs to be more variety within the schools system too. Some of the best schools have academic specialisations, which should be encouraged. It would be good to see federations and chains of schools emerge that offer different styles and methods of teaching. There needs to be a much greater emphasis on inculcating analytical skills, which are far better suited to a career in which people will change jobs many times. Cognitive skills are neglected and many children need to learn to be resilient, to be adaptable and to work in a team. There is no reason why some schools should not present themselves as being especially adept at helping pupils who have been labelled as difficult. Schools should be permitted to derogate from the national curriculum if they want to offer a significant stress on the arts or the sciences.

There ought to be some schools that extend the curriculum. The Sutton Trust has shown that pupils make two additional months' progress per year from extended school time and the benefits are greater for those kids whose lives at home are chaotic. At the Knowledge Is Power Program (KIPP) schools in the United States, pupils start at 7.25 a.m. sharp and finish at 5 p.m. On Saturdays the children are expected from 9 a.m. till 3 p.m. and they do three extra weeks of school in July. The kids are working, and so is the plan. The grades, in desperately poor areas, are superb, especially in maths. At least some British schools should follow suit and break down the academic year differently. The school year as we know it today was established in 1875 and has hardly changed since: three terms, each with a one-week half-term in the middle and six weeks off in the summer. The long summer holiday is a legacy of an agrarian society in which children were employed in the warm season as fruit-pickers. The National Foundation for Educational Research gave 1,000 pupils a reading test as they started secondary school in September and then compared the results with how the same pupils had performed in May. The fall in reading age would have given my mother convulsions. It is time to restructure the school year. Instead of three long terms with a huge gap in the summer, the school year could have five terms, each about nine weeks long. Terms would be separated by a break of a week. The summer holiday could then be cut to three weeks. The more variety, the better the chance of every parent finding a school that is suitable for their child.

That control is, though, an illusion if all the best schools are colonised by the wealthier parents. School choice is not real when money can buy places, as it can today. A 10 per cent improvement in Key Stage 2 results in a primary school brings with it a 7 per cent increase in local house prices. The extra payments on a mortgage in the catchment area of the best schools are just about equivalent to purchasing private education in the same locale. Wealthy parents are buying privilege, choosing to pay either termly fees or monthly mortgage payments in a market created inadvertently for their advantage by tightly drawn catchment areas. It is a basic principle that a parent should choose a school for their child, rather than have it chosen for them by the local authority. We need to reform the admissions process so that this is more than a hollow hope.

Most parents want their children to go to their local school. A quarter of all parents choose the school for their children on the basis that they can walk there. It would be ideal, of course, if all schools were good enough and therefore parental choice was less important. However, even if that is ever true, some schools are bound to be better than others and those schools will be over-subscribed. In those circumstances it is inevitable that not every first choice can be met. There then has to be a fair way of choosing which children get in. The usual selection device is proximity: the nearer to the school the child lives, the greater his or her chances of gaining a place. This has caused catchment areas to shrink to a tiny radius while school admissions officers walk the streets with a tape measure to work out which child gets in, and parents scrabble to buy the houses within them that come with guaranteed school places attached. This has, over time, been translated by an efficient market into a house-price premium.

Fixing the problem is easy but unpopular. The solution is to abolish catchment areas and allow parents to choose, in theory, any school they want. Free transport should be provided to give poorer parents the option of choosing a school at some distance from their home but in practice most will want to stay local. If a place is free in their chosen school then it should be instantly granted. When a school attracts more applicants than it has places it should explore the prospect of expanding. The admissions process could be brought forward six months, or more, to make this more practicable. But if expansion is not possible then we need a principle to distinguish those who get in from those who do not. That principle should be sheer chance: put the name of every child into a hat and allocate the places to the first names to be drawn out. The beauty of this process is that it respects parental choice and it is scrupulously fair. The lottery allocates equal weight to every child, regardless of the wealth of their parents. That is why it will be unpopular. It means that wealth can no longer buy advantage and introduces the lost principle of equality into school choice.

The Long-Term Condition of the NHS

A choice of school is one way in which citizens can exercise power against a bureaucracy. They can be given a guarantee of a certain standard of service with some form of available redress if it is not met. The best transfer of power, though, is the most direct. If people control the money then they can purchase what they need. Before the voice of the citizen can be heard we always have to ask, of every state agency: where does the effective power lie?

The best example of a revered institution with power in all the wrong places is the NHS, which is none of the three things advertised in its name. It is not national – local variations, in both provision and results, are too marked for that. It is not best described as a health service – the NHS does so little to apply the principle of prevention that it is more of an illness emergency service. And it is not, as its name claims, a single service. As Rudolf Klein says in *The Politics of the NHS*, this is a restaurant where one person orders the food, another one eats it and someone else again pays the bill. The Secretary of State sets the budget. The commissioning, planning and purchase of services is done by NHS England. Most of the money is passed on to more than 200 Clinical Commissioning Groups which buy services from the NHS trusts which, in turn, run hospitals and community care. The intricate avenues of the labyrinth are patrolled by bands of regulators and monitors.

The structure has evolved over time but the fragmentation was written in from the start. The founding fathers of the NHS established this separation of powers to ensure that, as with the American constitution, no single body could enjoy untrammelled power. When hospitals were nationalised in 1948, consultants became salaried staff in hospitals owned by the state. Primary care, meanwhile, was established in GP services that were constituted as private franchises. It can be hard to perceive where the real power lies in such a scattered organisation. A lot still rests in Whitehall and much of it these days sits with NHS England. Within the hospitals, despite the rise of a managerial cadre, the consultant doctors still hold the whip hand.

There was a logic to this structure once upon a time but that logic has gone. The district hospital is no longer the central location of the NHS. Routine problems such as hip replacements no longer require a visit to hospital. Victims of heart attacks, coronaries and strokes are avoiding death or disability every year because they are treated in small specialist units. Ultrasound, skin conditions and many other simple procedures are now done by GPs. Even chemotherapy can now be administered at home, and telecare means that patients can be watched without leaving their own bed. It might be the least popular campaign in the history of campaigning but we need to take to the streets and demand the closure of more hospitals. A&E, maternity, neonatal and heart and stroke care could easily be run from fewer specialist sites.

One of the most notable differences between *The Times* I was reading as a three-year-old and *The Times* I write for now is the coverage of healthcare. Lifestyle questions unknown in 1970 are now a staple of daily newspapers. Public health questions today are not, strictly speaking, public health questions at all, not in the way they were in Robert Peel's day. Public health was once about the eradication of noxious disease. The cholera epidemics of 1832 and 1848 killed 140,000 people. The solution was that the government – usually Tory as it happens – had to sanitise the urban water supply, which it did. Today's public health questions are less dramatic and more about moderation in behaviour. They are about our tendency to drink, eat and smoke too much, our sedentary leisure, labour-saving devices in the home and the less physically demanding nature of the modern workplace. Public health today is also not defined by contagious diseases in which the consequences fly through the air, infecting others. Though smoking passes on harm to others, the costs of eating too badly and drinking too much fall on the individual who does the eating and drinking. The upshot is the dominance of long-term conditions. Fifteen million people in England have a chronic condition for which there is currently no cure. The hordes of patients with dementia, diabetes, arthritis and hypertension are taking up half of all GP appointments, two-thirds of outpatient appointments and 70 per cent of inpatient beds. A quarter of all English children are obese and one British adult in twenty-five has diabetes. By 2035 it looks as if diabetes might consume 17 per cent of the whole NHS budget. For every £10 spent in the NHS at present, £7 goes on treating a chronic condition. Though the common wealth would start to prevent some of these illnesses in the next generation, we need to deal with the stock of current problems.

The most pressing of problems is social care. This is an issue in which the problem is acute but the solution is clear. The problem is that the costs of social care are visited on us capriciously. At some point in our later life, one in ten of us will receive a catastrophic visit from malign fortune which will cost us over £100,000. A further one in four among us will contract a condition which takes more than £50,000 from our savings. The current state of provision is a disgrace to a wealthy nation. The Equality and Human Rights Commission (EHRC) has reported that people have been left in soiled bedsheets for up to seventeen hours at a time and social care residents have been refused help with going to the toilet. Residential care is a quarter of the cost of a stay in hospital and care at home is a tenth of the cost, yet old people are stuck in hospital beds simply because there is nowhere for them to go. The 2011 Commission on Funding of Care and Support, led by the economist Andrew Dilnot, provided the answer that still awaits the politicians with the courage to implement it. Dilnot recommended that the poor should continue to be exempt and that individual contributions for the wealthier should be capped at £35,000. With certainty on that point a viable insurance market would be encouraged to flourish. The initial cost of the Dilnot scheme would be £2 billion a year. This is a fraction of the NHS budget of £80 billion a year and, in short order, the expenditure would be anyway recouped as so many patients would no longer be a burden on the NHS. An imaginative government would put aside the proceeds from selling the state's shares in the banks to finance the scheme through its infancy.

The answer to the travails of the NHS is to put Mrs Smith of Torbay in charge. Health services in Torbay, where eighty-year-old Mrs Smith lives, used to have an awful reputation. Mrs Smith staggered through the care system like Ariadne dragging a thread through the labyrinth. With every new meeting she had to repeat her life story. Stung by Mrs Smith's experience, Torbay's officials tore up their bureaucracy. The budget was organised according to her needs rather than those of the various fiefdoms of the NHS. It worked; emergency hospital admissions of the over-sixty-fives in the Torbay area were all but eliminated as the elderly were treated where they were most happy – at home.

There is an important fact to relate about the fabled Mrs Smith. She is fictitious. Mrs Smith is a character made up by Torbay's officials to illustrate the complexity of their system from the vantage point of a patient and how a transfer of power to the individual can improve the service. Baroness Campbell of Surbiton, a member of the EHRC from 2006 to 2008 and a campaigner for the rights of disabled people, once told a story that is a parable for an unresponsive state. Jane Campbell is unable to move unaided and so sleeps on a special mattress. When it got a puncture she sourced a replacement for £200 but was told the NHS would take care of finding the mattress. After several visits from staff, costly in themselves, the NHS concluded that Lady Campbell should have an extra-thick air mattress that cost £3,000. There was just one problem with it, which was that it left her lying a foot higher than her husband while they slept. It turned out that the NHS mass-purchase of mattresses was insensitive to Jane Campbell and her husband, who were told to sleep in bed at the heights the state ordained. Clearly, in respect of mattresses, the gentleman in Whitehall really lacks the faintest idea of what he's doing.

The way to give control to Mrs Smith and Baroness Campbell is to put them in charge of the budget, and happily there are signs that this is starting. By 2020, on the excellent plans set out by NHS England, 5 million patients will hold a personal budget which allows the individual concerned, in consultation with their doctor, to direct their own care. Patients with long-term conditions become world authorities on their symptoms and they are also in charge of administering most of their medical needs. They can arrange care that is appropriate and convenient for their needs, which they know better than anyone else. The NHS rates well in international surveys for efficiency but very poorly for being responsive to the needs of patients. The transformation in life chances, when people are put in charge of their own fates, can be extraordinary. To take just one example, a woman with a complex lung condition was provided with a machine to help her to breathe but every time the setting needed changing she had to travel to London. As soon as she got control of the money, she bought a variable-rate version that adjusted to her breathing pattern and she never had to go to London again.

To make the interests of patients paramount is not just the right thing to do in principle. It is also the only way to integrate the fragmented service. In any given health authority a thousand people, spread across fifteen professional cultures, would have to come together to produce an integrated mental health service. More than four-fifths of the services required to keep frail elderly people out of hospital are not, in any case, NHS services. Primary and secondary care have separate budgets, different access to data and workforces that rarely communicate. Yet achieving integration is now something far more urgent than a fond hope; it is a necessity. There is also strong evidence that integration improves the quality of cardiac, cancer and stroke care.

There is no prospect of integration ever being successfully organised from the distant centre of government. The NHS Confederation conducted a survey of the international evidence and concluded that integration derived from the attempt to cajole institutions into partnership yields no notable improvement to care. The only option is to grant power to the patient. Reform of the NHS can be a thankless task. There is a legend in the Department of Health that Aneurin Bevan's first act as Secretary of State was to get rid of the minister's lovely upholstered chair. 'This won't do,' he is supposed to have said. 'It drains all the blood from the head and explains a lot about my predecessors.' The NHS is the monarchy of the public services, a sort of solvent into which all rational criticism dissolves. But sentimental discussion of the service will impair our capacity to make it work and it will only work – it will only survive – if the patients are put in charge.

Contribution

Capable citizens who earn their own living and take control of their own lives deserve to have their contribution recognised. When a citizen has paid his or her stamps, to return to a language my grandfather would have used, he or she has earned the right to higher benefits than those who have no such record. Real need must always be met and a civilised welfare state is always a balance between the competing goods of need and contribution. But the balance of what people take out of the British welfare state has tipped too far away from what they have put in. The principle of contribution needs to be reinstated.

The lord of contribution is the most famous name in British welfare policy, Sir William Beveridge. In 1942, Beveridge famously had tears in his eyes as he greeted the request from Arthur Greenwood, the Labour Minister for Reconstruction, to write a report on social insurance. This was not a prophecy of the way his name would for decades live on as a paragon of welfare but frustration at being denied the job he craved, organising manpower on the Home Front. But Beveridge buckled down and, vastly expanding his given brief, sought to establish liberal principles of contribution and voluntary action as the touchstones of welfare policy. In the event, his 1942 report *Social Insurance and Allied Services* was an unlikely bestseller. Its sovereign idea was the contribution of the citizen. Beveridge always thought welfare should be 'first and foremost a plan of insurance – of giving in return for contributions, benefits up to subsistence levels, as of right and without means test, so that individuals may build freely upon it'. He therefore proposed a tripartite scheme of contribution, based on the more limited scheme of national insurance introduced in 1911.

As a consequence, Beveridge argued, general taxation should meet part – but only part – of the cost of any scheme:

Contribution means that in their capacity as possible recipients of benefit the poorer man and the richer man are treated alike. Taxation means that the richer man, because of his capacity to pay, pays more for the general purposes of the community. These general purposes may, and in practice they must, include bearing a part of the cost of social security; if security is to be based on the contributory principle, they cannot include bearing the whole cost.

Funding, in the words of the report, was to come from individual contributions. In his famous report Beveridge could not have been clearer: 'Benefit in return for contributions, rather than free allowances from the state, is what the people of Britain desire', he wrote in the report that bears his name. There was no appetite in Britain, he said, for what he called 'the Santa Claus state'.

Beveridge's original proposal was that individuals would be provided with a flat-rate income in old age that would be just sufficient to lift them above an absolute measure of poverty. This income was to be funded through contributions paid during a working life. However, the post-war Labour government wanted pensioners to benefit at once from the new system, and so chose to introduce a 'pay-as-you-go' system rather than a funded one; that is, they linked the generosity of pensions to the contributions of those of working age, rather than to the past contributions of pensioners. Furthermore, the original basic state pension (BSP) was not particularly 'contributory' in the usual sense; one's final benefit depended on the number of years of National Insurance contributions rather than on the level of these contributions.

The system was never wholly funded by contributions; state subsidies were needed from the start. But at their peak in the 1970s, contributory benefits accounted for 70 per cent of all social security spending. However, since then the principle has been eroded by all parties. Governments of the right tended to introduce greater means testing to help reduce costs. Mrs Thatcher abolished the earnings-related supplement, which meant that people with a strong record of contribution received higher benefits when they were out of work. Pensions now have no earnings-related component at all. John Major limited contributory jobseeker's allowance to six months. After 2010 the Tory-led coalition cut the contributory part of the earnings support allowance. There are plans, if they ever surface, to package all benefits, whether based on contribution or not, into a single Universal Credit. There was a time when Labour despised the stigma of the means test, which was, said Aneurin Bevan, 'a principle that eats like an acid into the homes of the poor'. Governments of the left have, however, increased means testing, in their case motivated by the desire to target help on the poor or to extend welfare coverage to women. That is why Labour introduced the tax credits regime, which, in the thirteen years from 1997, extended means testing from 13.7 million people to 22.4 million.

The big money saver of the current austerity drive has been the time limit placed on the last contributory employment benefit.

Whether the motive is to reduce cost or eliminate inequality, the upshot is the same, which is to erode the link between welfare and contribution. The increase in means-tested benefits has been dramatic. In 1979, a quarter of social security spending, excluding pensions, was subject to a test of means. By 2014, four-fifths was. In 1971, benefits based on contributions were 21 per cent of the total. Now they are only 5 per cent. Someone who loses their job and has paid their stamps for thirty years is only entitled to the same £67.50 a week unemployment benefit for six months as someone who has no record of work at all. Whether you have paid in for thirty minutes or thirty years it makes no difference. There is no reward for long service.

There is nothing ignoble about recognising urgent need and any welfare state will do so. But the British welfare state has taken a dramatically different course from the one intended and advocated by Beveridge and a different course from comparable nations. In Germany, the welfare budget is one-third funded out of contributions from the insured, a third out of employer contributions and a third from the pool of taxpayers' money. Unemployment benefit in Germany is split between a time-limited contributory benefit, available to all those who have paid National Insurance for at least twelve months in the previous two years, and an indefinite non-contributory benefit. In France, social security is financed largely by contributions based on the wages of employees.

The relegation of the idea of contribution has had the disastrous effect of eroding trust in the welfare state. The most recent British Attitudes Survey found that the number of people who think a life on benefits means a life of hardship fell from 55 per cent in 1993 to only 19 per cent now. The British people think that one in four welfare claimants is defrauding the system. The actual number is more like one in fifty. Thirty per cent of the British people think the poor have brought their misfortune on themselves. Across the world, there is a clear pattern. In countries, such as the UK and New Zealand, whose welfare states are based on entitlement and need, consent is declining and attitudes towards welfare recipients have become less generous. In marked contrast, countries with the strongest contributory elements, such as Austria, Norway and Holland, have seen no such decline. This is true even though their actual payments are higher. Consent is not about the amount. It's about whether the money feels earned or handed out.

A reinvigorated contribution has to draw its definition widely. To run a household is a contribution and so is to look after a child or to care for a sick relative. Older women do not have the same work record as older men. It does not mean they have made no contribution. Likewise, voluntary work is a contribution. Reward should not be confined to paid work and it cannot be beyond our wit to devise a system of reward in which these kinds of unpaid contributions are treated in the same way as paid work. People should be earning credit as citizens even though they may not be earning money.

As long as the definition is generous enough to recognise work of all kinds, then there is a lot that a government could do. First it would have to repair the paying-in side of welfare contribution. The principle of National Insurance needs to be defended, not collapsed into general taxation as Chancellors of the Exchequer are always tempted to do. There was no attempt in the coalition's austerity programme to protect contributory benefits. It could have chosen to revive employment or sickness insurance or devised a National Insurance fund to pay for social care. It did nothing of the sort. Then, on the paying-out side of the equation, people with a strong record of work could be given more unemployment benefit than those who do not. They could be permitted to jump the housing queue.

Contribution is an important principle that has gone missing from British welfare. It accords more closely with respect for fairness in British life than do more egalitarian conceptions of justice. This is a point that generations of people from the political left have struggled to comprehend. A strict egalitarian will not distinguish between benefits that are earned and those that are not. If the chief task is to close the income gap then money must be transferred from those who have to those who have not, irrespective of the previous flows. That was never the view of William Beveridge. As his biographer Jose Harris points out, Beveridge was furious at Labour's rush to state action and the crowding out of the voluntary associations which, as a Liberal, he was eager to nurture. In a little-known follow-up document called *Voluntary Action*, published in 1948, Beveridge lamented the damage that state welfare was already doing to the capacity of people to act unaided.

Public Service Ethos

In my dreary days in an investment bank, the only interesting point of the spread-sheeted week was the hour I spent, half a mile across the City border, in a primary school in a poor borough, listening to a young girl read. Or rather, trying to help to teach her to read, because the words came reluctantly. This was 1995, at the tail end of a long period in which basic standards of literacy in Britain had barely improved at all. Dredging from memory the method that my mum had used to teach me to read *The Times*, I made my pupil break down the sounds and blend them together. Fitfully, slowly, over many weeks, she progressed from sounds to words to phrases to sentences.

There is no reason why, apart from a tiny fraction of children with severe difficulties, every child in the country could not be taught to read adequately. This is a more stringent definition of literacy than simply being able to read. Fewer than 1 per cent of British adults are in that state. The pertinent definition is what is known as 'functional' literacy, which is to say an adult whose facility with the language is that which would be expected from an eleven-year-old. Something in the order of 5 million adults, 16 per cent of the nation, do not reach this standard.

It is a scandal that the number should stand so high. The four decades between the 1944 Butler Act and the 1988 Baker reforms were an experiment in seeing what happened when parents had very little power. The result was a mess. In 1995 the first ever primary school tests showed that two-thirds of eleven-year-olds went to secondary school unable to read, write or add up properly. I recall the Blair government setting a target for literacy to rise to 90 per cent. I remember thinking it outrageous, and I think it is outrageous still, that the government should have an official target for 10 per cent of the nation to be unable to read properly. A country can come together over certain objectives of which it makes a mission. Universal literacy should be the most important mission, the signature tune of the public services of the common wealth. This is a perfectly reasonable expectation. Canada has a literacy rate of 100 per cent, as do Finland, Norway, the Netherlands and South Korea. It's not about money either. Between 1971 and 2004 the US doubled how much it spent on education, with no impact on the national literacy level.

The decisive factor is priority. A nation has to decide that, in matters of schooling, its mission should be that all pupils can read. Eliminating illiteracy should be our national mission in the way that eradicating polio and TB was once. It is the equivalent of the Moon landings or winning the Olympics. A mission is as much about bringing the nation together in a common endeavour as it is about the completion of the task itself. Literacy prevents people falling into poverty and crime. It is the most important of capabilities. It is the basis of control. It is the foundation of a citizen's contribution. It is the point where all the principles of the public service ethos meet.

A child's score in a literacy test at the age of seven has been shown to be a very close predictor of lifetime earnings. We know, and it is not surprising, that poor reading ability at the age of ten is accompanied by, and exacerbates, low attainment across the rest of the curriculum, bad behaviour and inattention in class. In 2013 only 69 per cent of pupils reached the expected standard in phonics by the end of Year 1. About 100,000 children, one in five of the total, cannot read as well as they should by the end of primary school. This is, in large part, a story of the class system. The latest OECD report, which placed Britain behind every European nation apart from Spain and Italy for literacy, exposed a link between social origin and achievement that is stronger than anywhere else. Children on free school meals are twice as likely not to make the grade in reading at the age of eleven as kids whose parents pay for lunch.

It is all so unnecessary and all so damaging. I see no reason why pupils should not retake literacy tests until they pass. It matters that much. There is a programme called Every Child a Reader, which gives extra help to pupils who are falling behind. Its funding was cut and it needs to be restored, perhaps by using the Pupil Premium, which is supposed to act to close the education gap between the rich and the poor. The 1997 National Literacy Strategy, which forced schools to make literacy a priority, produced, after half a century of stasis, a remarkable improvement in basic literacy.

Not every child is fortunate enough to be raised by a mother armed with a copy of *The Times*. We all stand *in loco parentis* for those who do not. We cannot deprive any citizen of a skill so fundamental. To be able to decipher print on a page or squiggles on a screen is to shine a light into a new room. It is the skill at the very heart of a liberal democracy and the condition of its economic success. I didn't really teach the young girl in Tower Hamlets to read. I did nothing like enough for that to be true, unlike her teacher who had really done the work. But I was there when it happened and, no matter what little I did to help, I doubt I ever did a better day's work. I doubt too that I will ever see a smile like the one she gave me when the light went on and the words flooded into her mind and out of her mouth. The headline of a report from the Advertising Association Conference that appeared in *The Times* on 16 May 1970 put it well: 'plain speaking, new ideas make it all worthwhile'.

5

THE OPEN
SOCIETY

A Book of Common Prayer

My career break came through the 1662 King James Bible and Thomas Cranmer's version of the Anglican Prayer Book. At the age of twenty-one, I had neither experience nor knowledge of party politics and I had, almost by accident, applied for a job with a Labour MP. The advertisement had run: 'Frank Field MP is looking for an interesting, dynamic, go-ahead young researcher to set the political agenda for the 1990s'. Labour was Her Majesty's Opposition to a dominant Thatcher government and Mr Field wasn't even in the Shadow Cabinet, so the advertisement was stretching the truth a bit. I sent a card, with no covering letter and no polished curriculum vitae, on which I wrote: 'I am an interesting, dynamic, go-ahead young researcher keen to set the political agenda for the 1990s looking for a Labour MP looking for an interesting, dynamic, go-ahead young researcher to set the political agenda for the 1990s'.

Mr Field's secretary pulled out my postcard from the hundreds of more conventional applicants and I arrived at the Norman Shaw North parliamentary buildings for the next stage confident that there was no subject Mr Field could set for the examination that I was capable of answering. Fortunately I was wrong, because the set essay was 'What is the appeal of Mrs Thatcher to working-class voters?' To Labour activists of the time, Margaret Thatcher was a she-devil. To me, she was the Prime Minister my family happily voted for. I understood exactly what they saw in her. Mrs Thatcher stood, in their estimation, for self-sufficiency, work and contribution. The appeal of the market was not the freedom it offered but the discipline it demanded. There was smoke coming from the paper as I wrote all this down. I couldn't believe it was this easy. *Everyone* knew why Mrs Thatcher appealed to the people of Bury, didn't they?

My essay on working-class conservatism won me an interview with Mr Field at the House of Commons. As I write these words, the sense of awe I felt when I first stood in Charles Barry's Central Lobby comes back to me. I thought of the time my grandfather had come here as part of a delegation from the Bury Conservative Association to meet Walter Fletcher, MP for Bury between 1945 and 1955. And now there was I, in the denim jacket and Sta-Prest trousers I had unaccountably decided were the appropriate clothing for this interview. We walked down endless book-lined straight corridors to a room where we would have tea overlooking the River Thames.

It is known, I can now confidently report, as the Tea Room but I didn't know that then. Mr Field asked what were my interests outside politics, which was an easy question as I *only* had interests outside politics. Somehow resisting the temptation to talk about the life and works of Paul Weller, I told him I had been a choirboy in the Anglican church. That was the moment fortune arrived, at least for me. I had long sections of the Prayer Book by heart, and to Frank's evident approval, I expressed the strong view, which came unfiltered from my mother, that modernising the language in the Anglican Church was a kind of heresy. I had never thought, during all those years as a reluctant choirboy, that the ability to recall the Benedictine Creed would one day give me a break.

Yet it did, because the Book of Common Prayer was a shared experience which brought, for me, a job and, for Frank Field, an uninteresting, not very dynamic or go-ahead but at least young researcher. We connected through an institution which, at that time, defined a common life. Any political community needs binding; it needs a common idea of itself which is expressed through institutions to which we all consent. This is about much more than how we govern ourselves as a nation. It is about how we define who we are. Common institutions are implicit answers to the pivotal questions of identity: Who are we? How do we embody our public sense of our nation? What kind of nation do we wish to be?

This matters more than ever because politics, which used to have an economic explanation, increasingly derives from culture. British politics was once determin-istic. If you could establish that one of the two main parties was beating the other on economic competence and had a leader who was preferred as Prime Minister, their victory was certain. This compound held at every post-war British election, but in 2017 it stretched to the point just before it breaks. The Tories were well ahead on economic competence and, though both polled badly, Theresa May ranked slightly less poorly than Jeremy Corbyn. Even though the Conservatives just about won, there is one failsafe way to show that a quiet revolution was in train. With a Conservative Prime Minister safely in 10 Downing Street, Bury North returned James Frith, a Labour Member of Parliament. No more evidence is needed that something noteworthy is taking place than that Bury failed to predict the outcome.

Beneath the surface of the 2017 general election lay important cultural shifts. The lines of division are now less about how much we earn and more about who we are and what we think. Politics is merging with a sense of identity. This was evident in the referendum on Britain's place in the EU. Hostile attitudes to feminism, gay marriage, globalisation and immigration predicted, with almost perfect accuracy, a Leave vote. Anyone favourable on all four questions would almost certainly have voted Remain. These questions of value and identity, rather than class belonging, are increasingly coming to define political allegiance. In the two years between the elec-tions of 2015 and 2017, Labour increased its share of the vote among the ABC1 social groups by a remarkable 12 percentage points. The Conservatives had an identical leap among the C2DE classes. The electoral contest within social classes now is close. Politics has become much more about attitude and values.

This is in part a function of age. In the 2015 election, the pivotal age was thirty-four, which means that Labour won among the under-thirty-fours and the Tories among people older than thirty-four. Just two years later the pivotal age had risen to forty-seven. By 2022, on the current voting pattern, it will be fifty-two. Slowly, the people with closed attitudes towards the world are growing less and less politically salient. As people get older they tend to become more conservative, economically, but the same does not apply to their social attitudes. It is not likely that someone liberal on gay marriage at thirty will have become illiberal by the age of fifty. The Britain of the future will be liberal, diverse and cosmopolitan. It will not be the country of my grandfather, who was as conservative socially as he was politically. The battle in the common wealth will therefore be to defend an idea of the open society to which all can feel bound. The task is to construct a generous account of the British nation to which we all belong, to reform our institutions so that they embody that understanding and to describe the place of that nation in the world.

Forging the Nation

To do this we need to define the nation we are talking about and the simplicity of that question, in Britain, is deceptive. Britain is a strange tangle of nations which has a monarchy, a flag and an army but no football team. Each of Scotland, Wales and Northern Ireland makes a claim to nationhood but is not a state in its own right. The United Kingdom of Great Britain (England, Scotland and Wales) and Northern Ireland can feel like a contractual state-nation rather than a passionate nation-state.

Any attempt to define unique British values descends into platitude. Much as we might wish to compliment ourselves that Britain has a monopoly on liberty, equality and fraternity, we might find another nation makes a similar claim. To believe in decency, common sense and fair play does not distinguish Britain from those nations defined by their indecency, common stupidity and cheating. Neither do we get far by listing our private pleasures. My litany of national treasures includes, in no rank order, Victoria Wood, Philip Larkin, Isaiah Berlin, Emmeline Pankhurst, Lord's, Elvis Costello, Richmal Crompton, Chesil Beach, Alan Bennett, the West Pennine Moors, William Shakespeare, *Fawlty Towers*, city cathedrals and country churches, Elizabeth I, Billy Connolly, John Stuart Mill, P.G. Wodehouse, Sir Ian Botham, Helvellyn, W.H. Auden, Gareth Edwards, Mary Wollstonecraft, *Phoenix Nights*, Charles Dickens, Maureen Lipman, David Hume,

Manchester Town Hall and George Orwell. My list will almost certainly not overlap much with your own. I am conscious too that, though I come from a family that counts Ireland and Wales as part of its odyssey, this is a very English list. Those I cite who are not English – Billy Connolly, David Hume and Gareth Edwards – are Scottish or Welsh. Associations or institutions which are specifically British (summer-time, Library or Museum) are rare, though one such, the BBC, is a vital barrier against the tide of fake news online and ought to be defended stoutly.

Though it does not appear to mean much, Britishness does have a history. Linda Colley shows in *Britons: Forging the Nation 1707–1837* that Britishness was born out of Protestant disdain for Catholic France and the acquisition of imperial territory. Its purpose was to bind the Scots and Welsh into the Union and in that latter aim there is still a noble institutional purpose. Scotland, Wales and Northern Ireland are all more prosperous and secure as part of one nation than they would be as four alone but the case for the Union is more than that. There is, in fact, hidden generosity in an identity, such as Britishness, which on the surface appears to be not much more than a passport or the articles of association of a multinational state. To be British was and is an identity that Walter Fleischl von Marxow, the son of an Austrian wool-broker, could take on in his transition to becoming Walter Fletcher, failed parliamentary candidate for Frank Field's seat of Birkenhead and then MP for Bury in my grandfather's time. To be British invokes no kith and kin, no blood and belonging. This is why, although nine out of ten immigrants to Britain live in England, they tell pollsters that they feel British rather than English. The irony here is that British, the prefix of Empire, is the identity best suited to carry the idea of a generous, open, tolerant multi-cultural nation. But a British national identity forged by the institutions that allow us to live together well can and must be hospitable to all. The Britishness of the common wealth is a unique conferral of rights and responsibilities, exercised through and upheld by the democratic institutions discussed in chapter 3 of this book.

The Citizenship Test

A national identity that stresses democratic institutions is one that does not rest on excluding the wrong sort of person. The family that stretches behind me is drawn from the collection of nations in the state of the United Kingdom. The family that stretches in front of me is a small episode in the story of imperial adventure. There was a legend among my ancestors that the Collins family included Michael by that surname, the founder of the Irish Republican Army. I suspect the story is apocryphal but the Collins family did, nonetheless, hail from the Republic of Ireland. The Great Famine of 1845 stirred Peel to abolish the Corn Laws and my ancestors to emigrate to London. My paternal grandfather, Jimmy, grew up in the capital but, after he joined the Army to travel the world, he met and married my grandmother, Iris, who came from a small village near Cardiff. That was where my dad was born and, to this day, I retain an allegiance to the Welsh rugby team not lessened in passion by the fact that I was born and have always lived in England.

The family that stretches in front of me has an even more scattered origin. In 1933, a boy was born into a family in Moulmein, Burma, the third of seven children. The conflict between the Indians and the Japanese caused this family to flee back, on foot, to their home city of Madras, Tamil Nadu, south India. Sadly, both parents died soon after arriving home and, after a period of being looked after by aunts and uncles in Madras, the younger children were cared for by their heroic eldest brother, Hari. In 1962, at the age of twenty-nine, this third child left for England to complete his medical training. Though he always intended to rejoin his best friend Mani in the Indian healthcare system, he stayed and, today, at the age of eighty-four, he is in his fiftieth year of working in the NHS as a consultant radiologist. This man's children then sought their fortunes in British broadcasting and his daughter had the dubious distinction of marrying me. We try to ensure that our sons, Hari and Mani, are properly versed in the epics and the history of their Indian heritage which is a defining part of who they are. So is their allegiance, on which, as supporters of the Indian cricket team, they proudly fail a gormless test a foolish man once set. In 1990, the Conservative former Trade and Industry Secretary, Norman Tebbit, rather bizarrely used an interview with the *Los Angeles Times* to say that 'a large proportion of Britain's Asian population fail to pass the cricket test. Which side do they cheer for? It's an interesting test.' To which the obvious retort is that it is not an interesting test at all. Crass, exclusive and unBritish, certainly, but not very interesting. My children support India but they are, like their grandparents, British citizens.

It would be impossible for me to regard immigration as anything other than a good thing. But the case does not rest on my own biography. Now that the British-born workforce has passed its numerical peak and there is a larger body of retired people than ever before, Britain needs immigrants. For the first time since 1850 the over-all British population is growing faster than the available workforce. Immigrants are younger and more enterprising than the natives, more likely to be working and less likely to be drawing benefits. Importing labour has not been a cosmopolitan liberal choice; it has been a way of paying the bills. Yet the aggregate gains of immigration create losers as well as winners, and the loss felt is both economic and cultural. Lament for the loss of something familiar is the impulse felt in the northern mill towns, where Pakistani and Bangladeshi immigration changed the textile towns of Rochdale, Bolton and Oldham.

This presents government with an acute dilemma. A commitment to reducing immigration would impoverish

the country but an unimpeded flow of people ignites popular anxiety. The demands of identity politics and economic
need run in opposite directions. It is easy to cut immigration, if that is the only objective. Family entitlements can
be toughened up and fewer permits can be issued. It just
makes no economic sense. If the government ever succeeded
in hitting its immigration target, it would thereby harm
the nation. The only way through this dilemma is to
change the question. This does not mean we should change
the subject and avoid the discussion. On the contrary, we
need an open conversation about immigration in which we
talk about all the anxieties it raises. There *is* a tiny minority
of British people whose opposition to immigration is rooted
in prejudice. For the majority, though, 'immigration' is a
cover for fears about wage depression, welfare entitlements,
housing allocation, school places and job insecurity. Most
people who are worried about 'immigration' are not really
worried about immigrants. They are, quite understandably,
worried about themselves.

Anxiety about immigration will not start to recede
until illegal entrants are deterred and the borders are
well policed. The best way to achieve that is to give all
citizens an e-identity, a sort of high-tech identity card
which allows the tracking of people in and out. So long
as the data on the card is subject to safeguards about who
is granted access, there should be no objection to the
scheme. Identity cards are compulsory in over 100 countries, many of which − Belgium, Germany, Israel, the
Netherlands, Portugal and Spain, for example − are

hardly surveillance tyrannies. If, as a result, the government were able to tell the population, plausibly and confidently, that Britain had effective control of its borders then at least some of the concern over immigration would be mitigated. An identity card that, where relevant, contained a holder's visa status, would also prevent illegal working. Likewise, an entitlement to benefits or NHS care would be denied to anyone who could not display the relevant document. It would be no more onerous or intrusive than showing a utility bill to get a parking permit.

Reassurance that the borders are controlled will help to allay the anxiety that immigrants are taking all the jobs. In truth the robots are a bigger threat than foreign workers and the evidence that immigration has depressed wages is patchy, at best. It is probable, though, that black market, cash-in-hand wages have fallen to the competition of cheaper rivals. Wage regulation should be more consistently enforced and the National Living Wage should rise above the level of average earnings for every year of the next decade. This is a good policy for people in work, but more is needed for the next generation. Vocational education needs to be taken more seriously and the workforce better trained. British businesses prefer the higher skills of foreign-born workers and it is no wonder. The task is not to force their standards of service down. Vocational education is not considered an 'immigration' policy, but it ought to be.

With these changes in place, Britain should then extend its points system to all would-be immigrants, to select entrants whose skills the country most needs. There is no reason in these circumstances why the British people would not accept immigration which, it is accepted, the country requires. This system would include a national strategy for integration and a fund, such as existed until it was scrapped in 2010, to alleviate the local impact on public services. Mayors would expedite payment when local demands rise. Areas of high immigration should be designated as such and all people resident there a year or more should be granted a right to a place in one of their top three school choices. British citizenship would be a badge of entitlement which granted priority in housing allocation.

That preferential treatment would also apply to welfare payments. There is no need to pretend that welfare tourism is anything other than a myth. The idea of benefit tourism suggests that immigrants treat welfare states like holiday resorts, as if they go to the trouble of leaving family and friends back home for the irresistible allure of British housing benefit. The Migration Advisory Committee showed that migrants, younger and healthier than those who are British-born, are net contributors. Migrants as a whole pay 30 per cent more in taxes than they draw in the form of services. However, it is still, as a matter of principle, unfair that new arrivals should receive the same benefits as those who have contributed for years. If, as we saw in chapter 4, benefits were higher for those with a record of contribution, then nobody without such a record would be eligible. The claim that the undeserving were drawing from the system would be absurd. Welfare according to need makes no distinction between claimants from Birkenhead and Bucharest. Welfare according to contribution is a reward for citizenship.

The Great British Public

These are rewards that need to be earned and we should not be shy, in the common wealth, of expecting a level of integration. This is not an attempt to suppress pluralism. The good society will not appear because everyone suddenly converges on the same view of the good life. The only view of the good society we should be seeking is one in which people are given the private space to write their own scripts of what the good life means to them. There are two precepts on which we need to insist. The first is that, though in the private realm we are free to think, speak, dress and worship as we wish, there is a public realm in which we owe allegiance to democratic procedures. The second is that, as a citizen, our identity as a Briton must take precedence over other identities. British identity in the common wealth is defined according to our consent to democratic institutions.

The consequences of not demanding integration can sometimes be benign. For a time I lived in Stamford Hill in London. On one side of a main road lived the professional class. On the other, on a street called the West

Bank, orthodox Jews dressed for the eighteenth-century Polish shtetl inhabited their 'square of piety'. We lived parallel lives but perfectly peaceably. If two communities find a *modus vivendi* in ignoring each other, what need is there of integration? There is a great wisdom in this; where people are conducting their private rites and customs to the detriment of nobody else they should be given the space to do so. But a minimum level of integration is surely necessary because it is not always benign when people live in ways that never touch anyone from a parallel creed or kind.

When my parents split, my dad went to live in Heywood, a town half-way through the short journey that separates Bury and Rochdale. The prosperity that Heywood once enjoyed was based on the cotton mill opened by Robert Peel's father. In the mid-nineteenth century Plum Tickle Mill was the largest mule-spinning mill in the world. But the native cotton industry fell victim to cheaper imports and the town now makes its living from retail and manufacturing. There are twice as many people on incapacity benefit as there are in professional jobs. Heywood is a working-class ghetto town in which ninety-seven out of every hundred people are white. Three miles away in Rochdale, there are estates which are largely Pakistani. I used to play cricket for Rochdale Technical College, my dad's workplace; the team was Collins F. J. to open the batting, Collins P. J. at number eleven and nine Pakistani boys in-between. It worked as a cricket team, but cricket is a poor test of whether a place works. The schools are too separate and so are too many of the businesses. In a Heywood taxi firm in 2015, a gang of Muslim men were found guilty of raping a succession of vulnerable white girls. By their own testimony, these men regarded white girls as whores. They were women and they were white, two categories that relegated them from equal consideration. In the grip of a medieval conception of community these British Muslims felt that their primary allegiance was owed to a gross misinterpretation of the second term in that couplet.

In *Identity and Violence*, Amartya Sen warns of the danger of being defined by one dimension of identity. To be a Muslim, for example, is one part of who someone is but not the whole. That Muslim may also be a lawyer, a socialist, the son of a bus driver and the Mayor of London. Or he may be a banker, a Thatcherite, the son of a bus driver and the Home Secretary. Their identities are various; they contain multitudes. Religious devotion of course gives people a sense of who they are but it is important in the public realm that this is not their sole definition. There has been a tendency in recent years to describe people of Pakistani or Bangladeshi origin in Britain by their religious devotion. This happens much more often than Indians are described as 'Hindus' or English people as 'Anglicans' and it is a stereotype that needs to be resisted.

The same is true of the idea of race, which is a category that would disappear if we ceased to believe in it. This is not to say that racial discrimination does not take place. Black people are six times more likely to be stopped and searched than white people. Black children are three times more likely to be excluded from school than white children. The average prison sentence for white people was eighteen months in 2016 but twenty-four months for black people and twenty-five months for Asians. But look at the confusion in categories already. Sometimes people are reduced to skin colour, sometimes to a nation of origin or ethnicity or even, when very different people are labelled 'Asian', to a whole continent. The very idea of 'race' has no determinate biological meaning. Differences within each 'race' are far greater than they are between those groups. Much of what we ascribe to 'race' is in fact income inequality in disguise. A fifth of people of an 'Asian' heritage live in poverty in Britain while only a tenth of white British people are classed as poor. However, 'Asian' makes no sense, as Indian, Sri Lankan and Chinese families are considerably less likely to be poor than Pakistani and Bangladeshi families. Most of the difference can be traced back to education levels achieved in the country of origin a generation ago. It is hard to interpret along racial lines the fact that the worst performing children in school on reading, writing and maths at the age of eleven are white British pupils.

There are many candidates for the title of our primary loyalty – England, Islam, Jamaica, Bangladesh, Scotland, blackness, Leeds United, Catholicism, India, Wales, Yorkshire, Christianity, Asia, white skin, Manchester, Northern Ireland. But people will live together more harmoniously when our primary identification is with Britain. Nobody ever planted a bomb or wielded a machete to the rallying cry of 'God bless pluralism' or 'All hail John Stuart Mill'. To be a British citizen is, implicitly, to sign a contract to be a member of a democratic polity. It is to respect the institutions of such a state, which include the right of dissent. Indeed, the good news is that this is the country that has almost been achieved already. More than 80 per cent of people in Britain say they feel as if they belong. However, like the literacy target, this number is best viewed down the other end of the telescope. A fifth of the nation does not feel as if it belongs. This may well make Britain the most successful multi-cultural nation in the world but it is also not yet good enough.

Defender of Faiths

One way in which Britain is not good enough would have lost me the job with Frank Field. I retain a huge affection for the Anglican Church. I used to spend hours with my grandmother, the verger, in St Stephen's church in Bury, arranging the flowers for the Sunday service. My grandfather used to serve the communion wine. I never for a second had the fantastic notion that he was offering me the blood of Christ. It was sherry that my grandmother had bought from the Co-op and we both loved it. We loved the church and, in a remote way, I still do. I like to think I have invented a new category of the lapsed

Anglican. Yet there can be no justification, in a multi-cultural common wealth, which treats all religions alike and in which the separation of Church and State is the relevant article of faith, for an established Church.

Ever since 1535, when Henry VIII responded to Pope Clement VII's refusal to grant him a divorce from Catherine of Aragon by setting up his own Church, the ecclesiastical and the political have been joined. Church appointments in England are Crown appointments. The Church carries out state functions such as coronations, and the Lords Spiritual occupy twenty-six seats in the House of Lords. This is extraordinary residual influence for an organisation in precipitous decline. Between 1971 and 2007, the population of the UK grew 10 per cent. Membership of the Anglican Church fell 43 per cent. The congregation is so old — average age sixty-one — that natural wastage accounts for an involuntary annual fall of 1 per cent and attendance has now dropped below 1 million people for the first time. Like the political parties, the Church of England now attracts under 2 per cent of the nation through its doors each week. The Church is not exactly turning an attractive face to new recruits. An institution conceived in marriage is tearing itself apart on whether the privilege of matrimony should be extended to same-sex couples. By opposing women bishops, the Church has established the glass ceiling as a tenet of doctrine. It is no longer even true, as Larkin says in his great poem 'Church Going', that the church is the place in which our compulsions are recognised and robed as destinies. In 1950 two-thirds of infants were baptised. Today it is less than a fifth. Marriage is moving out of church and so is death. Churches are being turned into flats, bingo halls and curry houses. It is not ordained, to use an ecclesiastical term, that spiritual belief must rest in the Church of England. For every believer who is a church member, there are two who never attend. To describe it in phrases minted by Thomas Cranmer, Anglicanism is caught in the jaws of death, at death's door, given up for lost.

In a land of many faiths in which a quarter of all people told the last census that they have no religious affiliation at all, it is time to relieve Anglicanism of its connection to the state. Independence would let the Church pass its own legislation in the General Synod without the need for it to pass through the Ecclesiastical Committee of both Houses and receive royal assent. It could be freed from all public interference in the appointing of deacons, priests and bishops. Parliament does occasionally thwart the wishes of the Synod, as it did with the proposed reform of the Book of Common Prayer in 1927. The greatest prize to be won from disestablishment is liberty of religious conscience. Repealing the establishment of the Church would free Anglicans to marry only those of whom they approved because none of their weddings would have legal force.

Religious affiliation, in a multi-cultural nation, should also be taken out of education. Faith schools are the only state-funded institutions with a specific exemption from the Equality Act. Faith schools have 90 per cent of their capital costs and all of their running costs paid by public grant, and yet are still permitted to place restrictions on admissions, the content of the curriculum and school worship. It was once the case, but is no longer, that the Church was providing elementary education in areas of deprivation. These days, Church of England secondary schools admit 10 per cent fewer pupils eligible for free school meals than live in their catchment area. The other faiths are worse. The Roman Catholic schools have a deficit, on the same measure, of 24 per cent, Muslim schools of 25 per cent and Jewish schools of 61 per cent. This is academic selection on its knees in prayer. That intake, in which social class wears religious dress, is the clue to the academic success of faith schools. Faith is not a relevant criterion in education and the God before whom you kneel should have nothing to do with your children's education.

Magic and Daylight

The task for all institutions in the common wealth is to carve out the private space for differences by upholding a common life in the public realm. The Prince of Wales has tried to make the same point with his hope that, if and when he becomes King, he should be the Defender of Faiths plural rather than the Defender of the single Anglican faith. The point is an important one, because a

British identity that leans heavily on institutions really does need to be embodied properly. Public institutions need to speak for the Great Britain we are in the process of becoming, not the Great Britain that we never quite were. There is no revered institution in which the risk of looking backward is more woven into its fabric than the monarchy.

The monarchy could hardly have been more important in my childhood. I am named after my mother's hero, Prince Philip, and my sister is called Elizabeth. I rebelled against my mother's royal obsession even to the extent that I once wrote *The Man Who Would Be King*, a farce that played on the Edinburgh fringe, in which a radically free-market government tries to privatise the monarchy. Now it is not long before the man who would be King is crowned. Near the end of Queen Elizabeth's long reign we stand on the threshold of significant change to the way the task of monarchy has been performed. After a ruling by the Supreme Court, twenty-seven letters, written by the Prince of Wales to government ministers, were released. These 'black spider memos', known as such because of the Prince's untidy handwriting, reveal an heir to the throne whose conception of the task differs markedly from his mother's. The secret of Queen Elizabeth's reign has been silence. There is no better way to embody being above politics than to say nothing. This has allowed monarchy to be, as Vernon Bogdanor argues in *The Monarchy and the Constitution*, an effective shelter for liberal democracy. Queen Elizabeth's brand of monarchy has managed to gloss over the contradiction on which Bagehot gets stuck in *The English Constitution*: that the monarchy is, at the same time, both splendidly important and yet meaningless frippery of no constitutional account. It is obvious that a hereditary monarchy hardly embodies a common wealth based on work, merit and enterprise. The elixir of monarchy, though, is its adaptability. The monarchy has already gone from the sovereign power of the nation through the symbol of imperial grandeur, to the family of the nation and the welfare monarchy defined by good works. Today the modern cult of celebrity mixes with the ancient rites of monarchy in a compound made of flashbulbs and fairy dust, fickle fame and eternal truths. It is time that the monarchy underwent another adjustment. There are three sets of reforms needed – to finance, to ritual and to the way we honour achievement.

It is time to let daylight into the financial position of the monarchy. The Queen receives a Sovereign Grant from the taxpayer but the bulk of the family wealth comes from the Duchy of Lancaster, an investment portfolio whose exemption from corporation tax ought to end. The Queen is not required to publish private accounts but the distinction between the public and the private wealth of the monarchy is unsustainable. Before 1800 British monarchs were not permitted to own land but Prince Albert took advantage of the Crown Private Estate Act to acquire Balmoral and Osborne House. He paid for them by transferring public surpluses from the Duchy of

Lancaster, the Crown Estate and the civil list into his private funds. At that time, Queen Victoria did pay income tax, although she was relieved of death duties in 1894, a massively lucrative exemption. Then, in 1910, Lloyd George capitulated to George V's request to be let off income tax. Tax exemption for the Duchy of Lancaster followed in 1933 and, by the time of the Second World War, George VI was paying hardly any tax at all.

The system needs to be cleaned up. The Sovereign Grant should apply, as its name implies, to the sovereign only. The royal staff should be cut by at least half and the firm should turn a profit on its account by selling land where there is no security risk. The monarchy should be smaller and cheaper and its accounts should be published in full. The royal rules on financial disclosure, such as equity ownership, should be exactly as onerous as those that apply to MPs. There is no reason why representatives of the royal family should not be called before a select committee for scrutiny of the accounts. Then we should complete the slow task of making the monarchy truly above politics. The exemption that the monarchy has enjoyed from the application of the Freedom of Information Act should be lifted. Public servants are open to scrutiny as a matter of legislative principle, as they should be. This applies to MPs, councillors, civil servants, BBC journalists, police officers, teachers and nurses. The monarchy, though, is not mentioned in the protocol and it ought to be. The residual role that the monarch plays after a general election should be abolished. George V helped to select Lloyd George in 1916 and Baldwin in 1923. George VI was involved in Churchill taking the premiership in 1940 and the Queen had a role in 1957 in putting Harold Macmillan into Downing Street, and then again in 1963 with Alec Douglas-Home. It should not happen again.

Then the job of monarchy itself needs to be updated. The major reform is that the office should be for a term rather than a lifetime. Monarchs are likely to live longer than in previous eras and heirs are waiting for too great a proportion of an unproductive lifetime. The Poet Laureate used to be a job for life until Andrew Motion made it a post for a decade. The monarch should serve a longer term than that, but thirty years is surely enough. It goes without saying that, of course, daughters must become the equal of sons in line to the throne. In the meantime, while Prince William waits for the sands of eternity to recede and his turn on the throne to come around, he ought to go out to work. It was a mistake for him to give up his job as an aircraft pilot. 'Being a royal' is not a job. A common wealth founded on work and merit needs to be symbolised by a working family, and all members of the entourage should be expected to work for a living. The title of Royal Highness should be abolished and the expectation of bowing and curtseying should be abandoned.

These would be the first steps towards making the monarchy stand for the new common wealth. The next step is to invent some new public rituals. An open and tolerant democracy should not enact rituals irrelevant to our central idea of ourselves. An appeal to a counterfeit past is common in British traditions. When the Palace of Westminster burnt down in 1834, a Gothic pastiche was put up in its place. The horse-drawn carriage of royal occasions only became splendid with the invention of the motor car. Every royal occasion is marked by commemorative pottery Victorian in design, even though there was no pottery produced for Queen Victoria's coronation. None of the rituals we associate with monarchy actually draw inspiration from time immemorial. Queen Victoria's jubilee was invented on the spot by Lord Esher. The Duke of Windsor relates in his memoirs how Lloyd George made him say 'All Wales is a sea of song', in Welsh, while wearing white satin breeches. When, in 1969, Lord Snowdon wanted a script for the investiture of the new Prince of Wales, he wrote a new one. We should renovate our rituals once again, because that is what we have always done.

The place to start is with the honours system. The titles of the imperial past are obsolete now that there is no British Empire to be a Member or a Commander of. Some of the baubles on offer sound like jokes. The Most Noble Order of the Garter, the Principal Dresser to the Knights of the Thistle and the Yeoman Bed Goer are pure pantomime. The twenty-six civil servants of Permanent Secretary rank have no fewer than eighteen honours to choose from thanks to the different ranks within the Order of the Bath and the Order of St Michael and St George. There is even a Knight Bachelor and a Dame Commander of the Order of the Bath. This is before we even get to the political presents. Awards as egregious as Maundy Gregory's sale of honours on behalf of Lloyd George in 1918 or Harold Wilson's infamous 'lavender list' on his resignation in 1976 are rare, but the whole system needs to be more democratic and meritocratic.

It would be easy to make it so. The full panoply of OBEs, MBEs, CBEs, CMGs, KCMGs and GCMGs should be abolished and the Knights Bachelor and Yeomen Bed Goers retired. Instead of this complex hierarchy of half-remembered history there should be a single civic award, the Order of Merit, which announces the principle we seek to honour. There should be a companion honour for military distinction, the Order of Military Service, which would include commendations for exceptional bravery in combat. Then we should update the ceremony in which the anointed stand in line at Buckingham Palace for the entry of the Queen, accompanied by two Gurkha Orderly Officers and the Yeomen of the Guard. Currently, recipients are called forward by the Lord Chamberlain, according to rank, to receive their award while a military band plays. Anyone receiving the Order of the Garter at Windsor has to dress in a mantle of blue velvet, with a badge on the left breast, a hooded coat of crimson velvet lined with taffeta and a black velvet hat adorned with a plume of ostrich feathers. These old costumes are unhistorical fancy dress. The OBE was not actually invented until 1917. Honours in the common wealth would be awarded at a flummery-free democratic ceremony in Westminster Hall presided over not by the King but by the Prime Minister and the Speaker of the House of Commons.

Britain in the World

The image that Britain projects abroad is sometimes a pantomime version of its own monarchical past. In the new common wealth the reformed cultural institutions of Britain would convey a country that was modern, democratic and outward-looking. It would exhibit its system of government, its relative incorruptibility, its clean (if not always perfect) judicial process and its extraordinary array of cultural exports. Britain wields immense soft power from the credit shown in its philosophical, political, literary and musical balance sheet. The story we tell to the world should be the story we tell ourselves; which should be, in turn, the story of who we now are.

There are two other ways in which Britain can add to the stock of its moral capital. It would greatly improve this country's standing if we were to withdraw from the arms trade. No doubt less scrupulous nations would then take up the business but let them answer for that. There is no need to sell arms to regimes, such as Bahrain, Libya, Algeria and Saudi Arabia, which then use them against their people. Britain sent a delivery of naval spares to Argentina ten days before it invaded the Falkland Islands in 1982. In the six years before the Iranian revolution in 1979, the UK supplied 875 Chieftain tanks to the Shah. The Indonesian military in East Timor and the Zimbabweans in the Democratic Republic of Congo have fired guns with our name on them. It is not as if the arms industry is especially important economically. Only 0.2 per cent of the British workforce is employed in producing arms for export. The total arms trade accounts for only 1.5 per cent of total British exports. We should cease trading with states that do not pass a basic democratic standard. The world will not be instantly purged of terror because Britain stands on the high moral ground, yet if we are to preach the virtues of democracy in international chambers, the high moral ground is the only place we can credibly do it from.

The same is true of climate change. Britain is responsible for just 2 per cent of global emissions. A clean Britain offers little practical consolation if China and India and, in time, most of Africa pass through industrialisation the dirty way. However, that is no reason not to do the right thing. More engaged political leadership would do what none has yet achieved and make climate change a pressing domestic issue. The prevailing view has been the one that, in *Solar*, Ian McEwan puts into the mouth of Professor Beard, head of the National Centre for Renewable Energy: climate change 'comprised the background to the news, and he read about it, and vaguely

193

deplored it … But he himself had other things to think about.' It cannot be impossible to make the case that the lives of people on the flood plains in Bangladesh really count. Besides, the more oil we import for use, the more vulnerable we are politically to capricious regimes and economically to a spike in the oil price. Climate change puts British prosperity at risk.

Until now, climate change policy has lacked the grandeur it merits. Governments have stressed the need to be abstemious but carbon emissions will not be cut by unplugging the phone and giving everyone two bins. The little red lights can go out all over Europe and it won't make much difference. In policy terms climate change is an infrastructure project. It means that Britain needs to make a priority of renewing its nuclear capacity and it means proper funding for the science of prevention. The best warriors against climate change are to be found in white coats scribbling helix doodles, playing what McEwan calls 'the ghostly and beautiful music' of spectral asymmetry. The prospect of man-made climate change should inspire a drive to encourage a new generation of the civic-minded to understand that the most enduring way to change the world is to devise the technologies that will prolong the life of the planet. Low-carbon technologies are being developed that will allow us to electrify our cars, replace our gas-guzzling boilers and clean our power stations. The job of government is to devise incentives for this ingenuity, to impose a heavier tax burden on pollution and to seed the creation of as many jobs in the low-carbon sector as there are today in the NHS.

The prize for Britain, apart from the pleasure of living a cleaner life and respecting the planet's resources, is that we add ethical repute to our cultural influence and gain the right to be a moral leader in the world. This, though, is easy. Soft power only involves soft decisions. The really hard decision is whether to make Britain's moral suasion count in military affairs. The shadows of the wars in Afghanistan and Iraq hang heavy over any suggestion that this moral power should be translated into the harder power of military conflict, and Britain is in retreat. No longer a part of the major European alliance and a very junior partner to an erratic United States that, at a fever pitch never seen before, is itself going through one of its periodic bouts of exceptionalism, Britain is shrinking from the world. Retreat is a more or less conscious choice. Internal ructions within the Conservative party have tipped Britain out of Europe. Plenty of conservative voices can be heard to argue that the trouble-spots of the world are none of our concern. Labour, the party of NATO and the atom bomb, has been taken over by a cadre who believe that all shame in the world lies with America, the capitalist imperium. At the same time as Britain's will is declining, its capacity is receding. The Army is now no more than 80,000 strong, if that isn't the wrong word. Britain's Tornado fleet is a generation out of date and the Royal Navy is operating without a single aircraft carrier.

The world remains a place of some danger. There is a vicious civil war in Syria, with the tyrant Assad abetted by an unscrupulous Russia. Volatile states such as Iran and North Korea either toy with nuclear weapons or have them already. Countries that harboured brief hopes of democratic uprisings, such as Libya and Egypt, have returned to authoritarian rule. The Middle East remains as intractable as it has done for a generation and terrorist groups exploit any and every entrée into failed states. There are more than 50 million refugees, asylum-seekers and displaced people the world over. Meanwhile, economic power has been migrating east and, on the near horizon, the world awaits to see whether China ever harnesses its vast economic might for political gain.

There is a case to be heard for Britain forgetting past glories and retiring from a world role. Britain could become a kind of Denmark, with no great pretensions to international glory. There are plenty of advocates of this course but it is not one that we can afford to adopt. The idea that international crises can be contained within their own immediate spheres of influence is a residue of nineteenth-century diplomacy. Migration, the biggest issue faced by the EU, shows that a conflict in one region will wash up on the shores of another. The twisted ideology of terrorism is cultivated in the Middle East and then visited on the capital streets of Europe. Foreign policy is working much closer to home than it used to do. Even if Britain decides to retreat from the world, the world will not leave Britain to its own devices.

Besides, in this tumult it is important that the voices of the world's democracies are heard. When Britain speaks only *sotto voce* or not at all then the stage is left free for populist or authoritarian voices. Democratic sovereignty always wears a national garb. British democracy has unique elements. But there is also a powerful idea shared across boundaries which is that, everywhere that democracy is practised, the people are given a voice and the benefits of that power. If the large, powerful democracies – the United States, India, the nations of Europe – were to speak as one, their voice would sound the louder on behalf of a beautiful idea. Democracies do not go to war against each other. Nations that trade do not fight. Britain has a vantage point in the political chambers of the world and we will do ourselves, and our allies, a disservice if we relinquish that post. If we do not do our duty then power of another kind will take our place.

Though Britain should be conscious of its flaws at home it needs to be confident about its virtues abroad. An international order based on rules and consent is preferable to one in which might is right. An unflinching belief in markets for the public good, individual rights and the rule of law is an indispensable gift to the world and we should be wary because it is under threat. Nobody can be quite sure by what *force majeure* the world will be governed when China translates its economic weight into political power, but it will not be a system of order governed by rules. Britain is drifting out of contention in the world but we need to summon the confidence to turn back.

A Common Wealth of the Mind

The country of our imagination is not so far from where we already live. Britain has a tradition of dissent and democracy of which it can be justly proud. This is what defines the nation to which we all owe allegiance. The civic culture of the common wealth is not defined by musicians and comedians, of treasured landscapes and church spires. Britain's sense of its own special identity and Britain's privileged place in the world derive from the same source, in democratic procedure.

Though most of them need to be reformed and reinvigorated, there is a remarkable and durable account of a great nation in a list of defining British institutions that includes the impartiality of judicial process, the obligations of public service broadcasting, the fact that a man from Bury who cut his jelly with a knife could walk through the black door of 10 Downing Street, the laws of limited liability, sovereign power spread locally, nationally and globally, the support of the welfare state for the vulnerable, Manchester Town Hall, the sovereignty of the Queen in Parliament, the loyalty and courage of the armed forces, the principle of treatment by the NHS irrespective of personal circumstance, the Union of four proud nations, the best of the civil service, the splendour of the Central Lobby of the House of Commons, the unarmed police force, the membership of international alliances, the respect for public truth invigilated by a raucous press and opportunity for free expression, and the moving moment when the cars carrying the ballot papers arrive at the count, the verdict is entered and power is silently and peacefully transferred from one political party to another.

EPILOGUE

START
AGAIN

Back to Limehouse

There has been a Common Wealth Party before and its fate foretells what happens to small parties in Britain. In July 1942 Edward G. Hulton, owner of the *Picture Post*, the writer J. B. Priestley and the Liberal Member of Parliament for Barnstaple, Richard Acland, decided that the war effort needed a new party. Beginning as a social movement, with a strong critique of managerial capitalism, Common Wealth soon morphed into a political party that claimed to stand for Common Ownership, Morality in Politics and Vital Democracy. During the war years when the main parties had a pact not to contest vacancies, Common Wealth won three by-elections. However, that was its zenith. At its Hastings conference in 1946, Common Wealth split and became a pressure group, one of whose causes was the right for small parties to make party political broadcasts, before dissolving entirely in 1993. Having failed to become Common Wealth MP for

Putney in 1945, Acland joined the Labour party and was later Labour MP for Gravesend and one of the founders of the Campaign for Nuclear Disarmament. He then had one last go at breaking the mould of British politics when, in 1967, he provided the funding for the Labour MP Tom Driberg who, with his friend the American beat poet Allen Ginsberg, decided to form a new party. Driberg had the remarkable idea of trying to persuade Mick Jagger and Marianne Faithfull that they should be its figure-heads. They were intrigued and a few meetings took place before Keith Richards intervened to declare it the worst idea he had ever heard and effectively put an end to Jagger's political career.

Many years ago, on Mosley Street in Manchester, in the Central Library that A. J. P. Taylor described as a giant wedding cake, I researched a thesis into the brief period in 1934 when the *Daily Mail* endorsed the British Union of Fascists (BUF). Here was British populism, given institutional effect in a new political party, endorsed by a notorious newspaper in the first age of mass media communication. The putative leader of British fascism was Sir Oswald Mosley, the man whose family owned the land on which the library was built. Mosley believed he was the coming man of British politics, but in truth he was going nowhere. After spells as both a Conservative and a Labour MP and a job in the 1929 government, Mosley had resigned to found the New Party in 1931. After a humiliation in the 1931 general election, he turned the New Party into the gruesome BUF.

Most of the elements of forlorn attempts to create a new political party are contained in these short sketches. The initial enthusiasm and excitement, followed by the deluded self-regard of would-be saviours, the fringe philosophical dogmas, fratricide over nothing more than control, eccentric hangers-on and rank electoral failure leading to a humiliating withdrawal and a consequent splintering into ever-dwindling units. The undistinguished history of small parties in Britain contains many more unpromising examples than these but the one that hangs heavy over the whole enterprise is the Social Democratic Party (SDP). The meteoric history of the SDP begins in 1981 in Limehouse, the stamping ground of David Lloyd George and Clement Attlee, with the declaration of a split from the Labour party. For a time the SDP broke all the rules. At the height of its popularity, it commanded more than 50 per cent support in the opinion polls. At the 1983 general election the SDP won 25.4 per cent of the popular vote, but that was worth just twenty-three seats in a system that deters new parties. After a similar performance in 1987, the SDP collapsed in 1989 amid the usual, slightly comical, slightly tragic small-party wrangling.

The formidable barriers thrown in the way of new political movements are an incentive to remain within the current fold. In *Limehouse*, Steve Waters's play about the 1981 split, Bill Rodgers, the least well-known of the Gang of Four, breaks down in misery describing the break with his ancestral loyalty to the Labour party. He cannot be sure he has done the right thing in leaving. The answer to the anxiety is perhaps to point out that the successes of the Blair Labour party and the Cameron Conservative party owed a great deal, philosophically, to the positions struck by the SDP. Former members of the SDP were prominent in both movements. Perhaps this will happen again. The established parties each have infrastructures and a legacy vote. If the Conservatives can somehow resolve the contradiction between the nation-state and the free economy, their party could yet emerge from the intellectual doldrums of Euro-fantasy. If Labour can find a way to resist the temptation of revivalist socialism, its parliamentary social democracy might have a new vintage. It might, at a stretch, even be feasible for the Liberal Democrats to throw off the burden of coalition and challenge the prevailing order. There is no sign of any of this at the moment but, if any of the current political parties were to emerge as a viable carrier of the ideas of the common wealth, that would be a salutary turn of events.

This cannot mean, though, that the common wealth will be, in any way, an attempt to recapitulate political success of recent memory. The condition of Britain in 2018 is not a replay of 2010, still less 1997. Neither is the common wealth an attempt to reinvigorate what is sometimes known as 'the radical centre', after the phrase used by Roy Jenkins in *Home Thoughts from Abroad*, the 1979 Richard Dimbleby Lecture which is usually seen as the SDP's first salvo. Placing political parties on a spectrum that runs from right to left derives from the seating arrangements in the National Assembly of the French Revolution; loyalists to the right, dissidents to the left. This useful shorthand then locates a political centre. Any political movement more fiscally conservative than the Labour party but less so than the Conservative party will be described as centrist. So will any thoughts that betray a less ingrained distrust of state action than the Tories but more scepticism than Labour. This makes basic analytical sense but it is important to insist that fiscal moderation and judicious state action are *ideas*. They are neither right nor wrong because they split the difference between the two more extreme states of backward-looking conservatism and skyward-looking socialism. The common wealth needs to be founded on a principled prospectus, not an intermediate position whose co-ordinates are defined by others.

In Defence of the Common Wealth

The ideas of the common wealth which have been defended in this book are, in fact, hard to classify on a left-right spectrum and that should be seen as working to their advantage. The location of the 'radical centre', or any other political position, does not really matter. The common wealth is not a split-the-difference political fix. The common wealth is a philosophical idea which yields a set of political principles that are, in turn, embodied in signature policies. The first of these is that the common wealth is a market economy with a proper regard for the distribution of reward. It is a reinvigorated democracy in which power is returned to the people. Its public services will be organised to respect the principles of prevention, control, capability and contribution. It will be a society which is open and tolerant, in which a vigorous public argument can take place within institutions to which all citizens pay allegiance.

The common wealth takes inspiration from all of the traditions within British political thought. Its respect for established institutions and a fiscal discipline that is important when we are husbanding public money, derives from conservatism. It shares with social democracy a deep concern about the gap between the wealthiest and the poorest in the nation and a vigilance about the life chances of those who are not born into good fortune. Finally, it is an ideology of liberalism in the sense that it includes a spirit of dissent and discussion and an unquestionable tolerance for diverse peoples and ways of life. There is so much in British political history of which we can be proud. From the conservative tradition we can take Wilberforce's campaign to abolish slavery, Peel's advocacy of the consumer over the merchant class, Shaftesbury's Factory Acts and the public health and housing legislation of Disraeli. From the social democratic tradition there is the patriotism of Clement Attlee, the NHS free at the point of delivery and adequately funded services rooted in a deep respect for the public realm. From the liberal tradition there is David Lloyd George's desire to create a fair tax burden with the distinction between earned and unearned income, the welfare state of William Beveridge and the recognition, by Roy Jenkins as the Labour Home Secretary, that the law needed to change to allow people to live freely according to their natures. The common wealth is not an idea that is invented out of the abstraction of the seminar room. It is rooted in the heritage of the nation. The questions to which its principles are applied need constantly to be asked anew. Today, Britain is in the throes of an identity crisis about the type of living it will be able to earn, about how it can arrange itself fairly between people of different backgrounds and generations and about where it should stand in relation to the rest of the world.

In the open economy of the common wealth, the prospectus for change would alter the tax burden so that work was taxed lightly and wealth more heavily. Property would have to become subject to taxation, in part because that is fair and in part to fix a broken market in housing supply. A land value tax would be introduced and bequests would be subject to taxation. Companies would be expected to obey their public obligations and markets in which there are excessively dominant players would be broken up. Where automation threatens employment, profits would, in some way, be diverted to ensure that labour received the rewards that would otherwise flow only to capital. The living wage would be regularly updated in excess of inflation so that the least well-paid kept touch with the best.

The politics of the common wealth would be revived by locating power as close to the people as possible. Local government would be granted more revenue-raising powers and the experiment with metropolitan mayors and city government would be extended. The civil service would be reformed to make it slimmer and more dynamic. The electoral system would be reformed to make it fairer and more proportionate and voting would become compulsory. The House of Lords would, finally, be included in the list of democratic institutions chosen by the popular vote. Political parties would be recognised as the vital bodies they are by the receipt of public funds. The authorities of the law would work more effectively to promise the security for citizens which is the foundation of their freedom.

The effective use of public money, on behalf of the sovereign people, underpins the provision of public services in the common wealth. Those services will be organised with four principles in mind: prevention, capability, control and contribution. Public spending will be oriented systematically towards the earlier years of life, where returns are highest. There will be, in the common wealth, a concerted effort to prevent problems such as drug abuse and long-term health conditions before they arise. The capability of all citizens will be enhanced by a curriculum that respects the variety of talents. A serious vocational curriculum will be established and public examinations at the age of sixteen abolished. Lotteries will be introduced into school admissions to make the process fair and a range of schools will be encouraged, some of which will vary in their teaching styles and content and not all of which will retain the traditional school year. Parents, pupils and patients will be given power in the common wealth public services. Control will take different forms appropriate to each service; sometimes it will be a simple choice, on other occasions the recipient of the service will help to design what they receive and, where appropriate, they may control the budget. The contribution of citizens will be noted with extra benefit payments due to those who have a record of service.

This is the basis in policy of a common wealth that is an open and tolerant society with an identity rooted in appreciation of British democratic institutions. In such a society immigration will be valued for the contribution of its new citizens. Its impact on the host society will be mitigated with a fund for public services and the root causes of hostility to immigration, which is not at all the same as animus against immigrants, will be addressed. Borders will be controlled and an e-identity card introduced. Allegiance to institutions in the public realm is the indispensable counterpart to tolerance of all lifestyles in the private realm, so those institutions need to be reformed so that they stand for the nation that Britain is today rather than the nation it used to be. In the common wealth the Church of England will be disestablished, the rituals of monarchy updated and the honours system brought out of the lost imperial mist. This will project a modern image of Britain at home which should be mirrored abroad in a nation that is a confident actor on the world stage, a participant in international alliances and one of the democratic guarantors of a rules-based world order.

Taken as a whole, the ideas recommended in this book point towards the just society of the common wealth which is a nation we should be glad to call home. Weary experience of British politics might suggest that this is a utopian longing. Small parties need a miracle to break through and arrival at the island of utopia always requires a journey through the sea, a time machine or the sleep of transportation. J. B. Priestley, one of the founders of the Common Wealth Party, used a theory known as a time slip in his play *An Inspector Calls* which places the emphasis on the importance of pre-cognitive dreaming in which we see the future in outline. It is often said that the hope of a new political movement is like this. However, there are reasons to suppose that the sorry saga of small parties need not necessarily repeat itself. There are definite grounds for dreams and for optimism.

Britain has not given the Conservatives a working majority for thirty years. Apart from its leader *non grata* Blair, Labour has not won a victory of any description for forty-four years and has not had a decent majority since England last won the World Cup. This is not two-party politics, it is none-of-the-above party politics. These are not parties that can dominate politics properly now and the conditions are not as inhospitable as they were in 1981. When the SDP broke from Labour, the Conservative party was only two years into its time in government and the economic cycle was about to turn in its favour. In 2018 a tired government has been in office, in three separate incarnations, for eight years and the economy is in peril of a recession. In 1981 the Conservatives were run by the right wing of their party and Labour by its left but Mrs Thatcher's leadership, which proved to be strong, was seen as a response to the still-resonant crisis of 1978. None of that is true now, when neither party appears able to break the stalemate.

At the same time, there may be something more fundamental going on. The extension of the franchise to working-class men in 1918 and then women in 1928 helped to usher a new party, Labour, into being. There is no extension of the franchise now but people are certainly voting differently. The electorate is not growing but it is changing because, as we have seen, the historic link between class and political affiliation, which has been weakening for a long time, seems to have broken. The political descendants of my grandfather – working-class people voting Tory – are now more numerous than they have ever been. Labour, meanwhile, is slowly becoming a party attractive to the metropolitan bourgeoisie. The European referendum of 2016 has interrupted the usual voting pattern. Politics after a major referendum, in every country that has ever held one, is always volatile. It is always a moment in which strange things happen. Control of the two main parties is more securely held by their extremes than it was in 1981 and the shifting absurdities of the negotiation to leave the EU are stretching party ties. Europe could yet be the catalyst of significant changes to party politics as well as to the nation those parties aspire to govern. Look at how the Labour party collapsed in Scotland. Identity politics wiped a party out; all that was solid melted into air.

These are the circumstances which have caused an epidemic of political homelessness. This book is a call to those people who do not feel that politics today is speaking to them. It is written in the belief that they are plentiful and that they are deeply frustrated with the current dispensation. It is, of course, hard to break such an entrenched political system and it is easy to give way to fatalism. So let us instead concentrate on the demand rather than the supply. Imagine that there was a new party, or that one of the main parties freed itself from its ideological cul-de-sac and took up the ideas of the common wealth. Suppose that this party were staffed by experienced campaigners from all three of the main parties but were to attract new people into politics too and engender a sense of excitement and novelty. Do you not suppose that this party would do well and that the residual, existing parties would be scared of it? Would you not, yourself, be tempted to vote for it?

The purpose of this book has been to supply that impulse with ideas and thoughts about how this country might be improved. It has sketched the outline of a patriotic common wealth which has more vitality than anything on offer from the two main parties. It has laid the ground for an open society in which stories of social mobility will be possible again. It tells the story of how we can fix British politics, which is plainly broken. All we need to do is to start again.

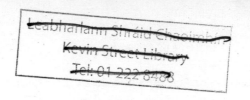

ACKNOWLEDGEMENTS

A book of this kind, much like everything else I do, took somewhere between three months and thirty years to write. During that extended period, I have accumulated more debts, political and intellectual, than I can hope to repay here. I have learnt as much from political opponents as from fellow travellers and more from failure than from success. The search for a viable political course has taken me from left to right and back again and somewhere in the mix, though not necessarily in the middle, I think there is an attractive prospectus. To all those who have contributed along the way, my thanks.

Two institutions helped me hugely too, largely by paying me to do work I would have paid to do. It was a great privilege to work in 10 Downing Street and the same applies in the present tense to *The Times*. I am hugely grateful to all those responsible for the opportunity afforded to try out some of these ideas, first in practice and then in print.

For their forbearance, love, companionship, critique and proofreading, my deepest thanks are due to my family. This book is, I hope, infused with a sense of place and it is my family who keep me in mine.